Ready or not…

Here she comes front and center, live and in-person – Mrs. Shelly Lockett, a true woman of God who I have the pleasure of knowing for 10 years.

During that span of time, I have witnessed firsthand her natural ability to communicate and interact with people of all ages, social statuses and backgrounds in a sincere, direct and compassionate manner without compromising her integrity and values.

Mrs. Lockett is a spirit-filled, full of faith and courageous woman whose presence, faith and discernment "kept" me during my tenure as Board President at KIPP Endeavor Academy and inspired our leadership and staff to accomplish what was seemingly impossible!

Personal Character

As I reflect back to when I first met Mrs. Shelly Lockett in May 2010 to the present, three words come to mind – Reliable, Determined and Virtuous.

- Reliable – When other administrators and teachers elected to vacate or shun their responsibilities during the school restructure, Mrs. Lockett maintained her focus and commitment to the students to be a person of standard that students could count on in a time of turmoil and transition.

- Determined – She had an unwavering commitment to hold the school leadership, teaching staff and the board accountable to actively participate and establish a culture of academic enrichment needed to enhance the lives of urban youth inside and outside of the classroom.

- Virtuous – Her innate ability to discern and embrace God's vision for her life and exert the energy to pursue opportunities to enable God to fully utilize her gifts and talents is amazing.

For those who read this book, I fully expect their hearts to be encouraged, their spirits challenged and their hearts to be forever changed by this godly woman whom I affectionately call Mrs. Lockett!

Anthony D. Williams
Kansas City, MO

It is a privilege and honor to introduce my cousin and lifelong friend, this woman of God, Shelly Lockett, to the millions of readers I pray will be blessed by *Sharpen Your Sword: 50 Inspirational Parables To Make It In Life.*

I believed at an early age that Shelly was different, set apart in her family, and chosen to accomplish great things to bless you and me. As I look back over her life, I realize she is a true example of the saying, "what doesn't kill you makes you stronger." Her contagious smile lights up any room, capturing the heart of many people. As you read her book, you will wonder how she got over everything she's experienced. Let me tell you first-hand: it's God's amazing grace. In spite of it all, she is still standing tall. Shelly uses the good, the best, the bad, and the ugly to empower all of God's people she has been assigned to, whether family, friends, or strangers.

I remember to this day when we were little children at Grandma Birdie's house, and Shelly said to me, "Nessa," (as she affectionately calls me) "one day, I will write my story; I want to be a blessing to so many people." I believe she's doing exactly that with this book. She has inspired me to be the best me I can be.

Let these words encourage you: you can do all things through Christ who strengthens you (Philippians 4:13). There is nothing too big or too hard for you. God has given you 50 inspirational parables in this book to help guide you. These are the words I leave with every reader: when it's all said and done, after this book blesses you with a breakthrough in your life, remember to return a mighty thank you to our sender above, God. Now, pick up your sword and sharpen it, for our defender, Jesus, goes before us.

Vanessa Brown-Redwood
Cousin and Lifelong Friend

From the early days of childhood, our mother has always been a spirit-filled dynamic woman of God. She would affectionately wake us up, singing "Rise, Shine, Give God the Glory," modulating each time until we woke up for the day. The importance of starting each day off with God was emphasized in more ways than one. As we continued to mature, our parents would teach us through weekly family Bible study nights. All three of us remember the massive white book, which read "Family Bible" and contained a plethora of Bible stories with magnificent illustrations.

These days she constantly reminds us that she's "holding on to King Jesus" and continues to model what a true Christian should look like. Our mother has kept us lifted in prayer, admonished us with biblical teachings nearly every day, and stays in awe of the magnificence of God, even in the little things. Her deepest desire is for each of her sons to develop and maintain a personal relationship with Jesus Christ, so by the time you read this, each one of us has already received copies of this book and has had conversations about the inspirational parables throughout the writing process and beyond. As you read this book, we want to leave you with a gem that our mother has imparted with us: "Only what you do for Christ will last." We love you, Mom, or Evangelist Lockett, as many of you may come to know her!

May this book help you continually refine your walk with God as we all strive to navigate this life and prepare for the next.

Your Sons and Daughter,
Marcus, Brae, Juwan and Javon

SHARPEN YOUR SWORD

50 Inspirational Parables
to Make It in Life

SHELLY LOCKETT

Favor Management, LLC

LEE'S SUMMIT, MO

Published by Favor Management, LLC
Lee's Summit, MO
For permission requests, email favormanagement21@gmail.com
For more information, please visit: ShellyLockettMinistries.com

Editing and Interior by Rachel L. Hall, Writely Divided Editing and More
Cover by BetiBup33 Design Studio, http://thebookcoverdesigner.com/designers/betibup33/

ISBN: 978-1-7368687-0-6 Paperback edition
ISBN: 978-1-7368687-1-3 eBook edition

Sharpen Your Sword: 50 Inspirational Parables to Make It in Life / Shelly Lockett — 1st ed.

Dedication

I dedicate this book to my Father God in Heaven, who never gave up on me and could see all that He placed in me from the beginning.

To Jesus, for dying on the cross for my sins and saving my soul.

To the Holy Ghost, for never stopping to teach me, even when I didn't listen.

To my mother, Teresa, known as Tressie, and my dad, Herschel Jr., both of whom never lived long enough to see what all my Father God was doing in and through me.

To my caring husband Jeffrey of 26 plus 3 bonus years—you are one of the nicest men I've ever met, and you have never made me feel abused or ashamed but spoil me every chance you get.

To my three princes, Marcus, Juwan and Javon—you gave me some special years to look forward to as a young woman, and you allowed me to be your mom unconditionally. You each have a special undeniable love for me that propels me to pray to God to reveal Himself to you more and more, as He has with me. I thank God for allowing you to feel His love through me, for sparing your lives and for covering you in spite of life's hurts, harms and dangers.

To my daughter-in-love, Brae—you have not only birthed two of my most precious grandchildren, but you have also contributed to my growth as a mother because before you, I did not have a daughter to truly call my own.

To my three grandchildren that affectionately call me Grammy, for "award-winning grandmother," that after all I've endured, if I don't get a Nobel peace prize down here, hopefully, my mansion in heaven will be right next to God's and I will be allowed to lay at His feet daily. I love you three with the heart of God. Daniel "DJ" James, Kamryn aka Kammie, and Jai Anthony, I smile with sincere joy that God has favored me so much to have three of the most beautiful grandchildren in the world. I pray that in time if God delays Jesus' return, this book will inspire the three of you to live your best, blessed life.

To my sister Vantish, who taught me what a real giver is, to my brother-in-love Fredric, and to my big, little brother Phil (as I laugh).

To all of my relatives, the Garvins, Clarks, and Hollinsheds, my mother-in law Jinnie Lockett, my brother-in-law Gary and his wife Donetta, and my brother-in-law Millard. A special acknowledgement to my Aunt Louise & Uncle Kevin, Aunt Veola, Uncle Alonzo, Aunt Charlotte, Aunt Alice & Uncle Chuck, Aunt Carolyn, Aunt Rubie, Aunt Babe Ruth, Aunt Georgia, Aunt Marie, Aunt Rosemary, Aunt Shirley, my cousins Joe, Deidra & Elgin Sr., Patricia & Nukes, Crystal & Jay L, Bev & Charles, Ed & Yolanda, Anthony & Cynthia, Janice & Kyle, Tony & Shaunta, Clarence & Carla, Gwendolyn, Rodney, Harvey Jr.,

Sheila, Stephanie, Sheeky & Andre, Leron & Lucretia, Ra-Shawn & Terrence , Ra-Chelle & Michael, Ra-Keish, BJ & Melissa, Quante, Tiffany, Butter, Terry, Marchetta & Calvin, Anitrea, Lamont, Terez, Rissa, Damian, Poppy, Star, Mia, Jordy, Erica, LaShaun, Marvin Jr., Danielle, Briana, Josh and Michael: I love each of you. To all of my relatives, aunts and cousins near and far—too many to name, but know that I love you. For those that attend family reunion, I live to please you and make sure that each one is more memorable than the last. To special friends Susie and Mike Sims Sr., Kimmie and Reggie Young, Melanie and Randolph Cobbins, Carrie and Jesse Moore, Sherry and Gregg Sanders, Jeffrey and I love you guys so much.

To my Trinity Temple COGIC church family, St. John MBC church family and New Hope COGIC church family.

To my dearest grandmothers, rest their souls—Maggie Quintella Scott, my great-grandmother who read the Bible to me from the time I was four years old and Alice Verser-Hollinshed, my paternal grandmother. I would listen at her door as she prayed: it sounded like Jesus was in the room with her. Through her example, I've learned to pray exactly the same way. I'm sure both have a mansion in heaven somewhere along the golden streets. To my grandmother, Birdie Lee, who I thought was too hard on us. Now I understand what she was shielding us from when she made us get on the porch before the streetlights came on and to come in the house when they did.

To my pastor, Bishop Dr. Benjamin Stephens III and my First Lady, Supervisor Dr. Latonya Stephens. I want to be a better version of myself by watching you. You both carry and live the gospel the way God intends for pastors and their wives to do it. To Lady Stephanie and Elder Terry Bradshaw Sr., and my previous pastoral leaders, I pray I make you all godly proud.

To my lifetime friend and cousin, Vanessa Brown-Redwood. You have been there in spirit and in presence. You know my strengths and weaknesses and you have never denied the power of God's presence in my life. You have prayed for me and witnessed me marry the love of my life twice in 25 years.

To my business colleague and friend, Mr. Anthony Williams—you taught me the meaning of being a professional businesswoman and how to get people's attention without seeming like an angry black woman. Which, by the way, you know I never was, but simply always straightforward and to the point. (I smile thinking of you and the business bond we built.)

Last but certainly not least, may all who read my book sharpen your spiritual sword and feel the love of God guiding their lives to live each day with a fierce passion to get to know Him more and more until eternity.

Passionately,

Shelly E. Lockett

CONTENTS

FOREWORD

BY BISHOP BENJAMIN STEPHENS, III
& DR. LATONYA STEPHENS

For a believer, life can be a daily battle. God gives every believer a sword to defend themselves against the wiles and schemes of the devil. Our primary weapon of warfare is our sword, the Word of God, also known as the Bible. Committed Christian soldiers would agree: one's sword should always be present and sharp.

Life presents a myriad of ordeals and obstacles through which the believer must exhibit faith in God. Paul exclaims in the book of Romans that faith comes by embracing one's sword—the Bible. A swordsman's success is found in being proficient at swinging their sword to defend, deflect, and discern the enemy's attacks.

Swordsmen must become one with their sword to be effective. The demand for a sharpened sword is vital and imperative, to say the least, for spiritual survival. Every believer must strive to merge scripture into their daily lives. The sharpened sword not only protects the believer but enhances their relationship with God. Maintaining a sharpened sword demands a lifestyle of discipline. An exquisitely sharp sword must be handled with care, taken seriously, and always carried faithfully. To be a productive Christian, use your sword!

The absence of one's sword can be detrimental. Many believers become lukewarm as they lay down their swords for the sake of convenience and compromise. Many Christians become too comfortable as they neglect their sword by taking it for granted. When a sword is not used for an extended period, the blade becomes dull and ineffective.

I have been privileged to observe some extremely decorative swords. The significance of a sword is not in its presentation but its execution. A sword's appearance can be deceptive because you never know exactly how sharp it is until you engage or encounter the blade. A dull blade is counterproductive if you seek to establish a quality relationship with Christ. The believer's sword (the Bible) should be engaged daily, but many neglect their sword, allowing it to collect dust on a nightstand or take up space on the countertop. Those who remain consistent and committed to sharpening their sword will have spiritual success.

Growing up as a kid in church, we would play a game entitled "Present your Sword." The object of the game was to see who could find a scripture the fastest. Youth leaders of yesterday encouraged us to familiarize ourselves with the Word of God. I fell in love with my sword, so much so that I made a career of swinging, sharing, and sharpening my sword. Due to my rearing in the Church of God in Christ, I carry a sharp sword, and there is never a day that I do not have to "Present My Sword," whether in my personal life or public ministry.

I know that this book will bless you as you endeavor to *Sharpen your Sword!*

Bishop Benjamin Stephens, III, D. Min.
Trinity Temple COGIC, Senior Pastor
Vancouver, Canada Ecclesiastical Jurisdiction, Prelate
Lee's Summit, MO

To know Shelly Lockett is to know that she LOVES God! She often shares nuggets from her life experience, and she always lets you know that she is "holding on to King Jesus!" The humorous approach she has to engaging others in person is conveyed in her writing. When I first met Evangelist Lockett, I did not know I was being introduced to a woman of such strength, courage, warmth and humor. She is an evangelistic comedian with a giving heart who offers layers of herself through inspirational messages, servanthood, and prayer. She provides practical advice and real-life stories to which many can relate.

There are many self-help books available, but what I like about this book of inspirational parables are the serious but light-hearted approaches to life-changing solutions to escape drama and bad decisions. Shelly writes, "Bad advice is like bad breath! Nobody wants it!" She made me think. It is amazing how some loquacious individuals are unable to detect that their breath is bad. It can be so bad that I am willing to walk away from a good conversation for a moment of freedom. The analogy of bad breath and bad advice reminds us to walk away from things that can leave a stench in our lives or that are a stench to God.

Isaiah 50:2 reminds us that without water, fish stink, then die. Accepting bad advice is similar. It is like trying to drink from a dried well or river when we are thirsty. It leads to dehydration, then eventually death. Two ways to combat bad breath are to avoid a dry mouth and change your diet. We can simply ask God to give us an ear to hear as the learned so that we may discern the difference between bad or senseless advice and wise counsel. If we have been guilty of providing bad advice, then we can ask God for wisdom and the tongue of the learned, so we will know how to uphold the weary soul with words that are uplifting and on time.

As you read this devotional, get ready to change your diet. Change how you perceive the world, change what you hear and accept. Change how you think. Last, but not least, let's change what we inhale—especially bad breath.

Dr. Latonya Stephens, PhD
Trinity Temple COGIC Worship Director
Supervisor of Women
Zambia Second Jurisdiction COGIC
Lee's Summit, MO

A Letter &
Testimonial from
the Author

I've been up and I've been down. I've been in the place where I've been abased and I've been where I abound. I've lost everything and gained it back. I've thought about committing suicide, attempted it once, and God wouldn't let me die. I've been molested as a little girl, left afraid and felt ashamed of myself for it. I was scared of men because of it and wanted to go the other way due to it.

One day on the highway, the car I was riding in began to spin out of control. When it came to a halt, it was facing the oncoming traffic. Suddenly, all traffic stopped, the clouds opened up, and the Voice of God said, "You're heading the wrong way. This is not the plan I have for you." That day, at age 18, I was delivered from a demonic attack on my womanhood. In light of this, I know that God has not given His authority or permission to any alternative lifestyle. If you're reading my book and practicing any lifestyle other than what God approves, please know, He loves you dearly and wants me to let you know you're heading the wrong way. Turn back!

I faced my attacker via telephone after he had the audacity to ask to speak to me while happenstance being in the same prison my brother was visiting. I got the chance to congratulate him on finally getting what he deserved: prison time for molesting other little girls like me (he had gotten away with molesting me). My prayer is that those little girls never faced the self-shame and blame I placed on myself.

I turned to drugs to try to mask the anguish of an early life of pain. I sold drugs to finance a dream lifestyle—with no gain. I fell just short of complete despair. Somehow, I knew God was still there. I could hear my grandmother's voice. When I was a young girl, she would say, "Baby, if you ever lose your way, Jesus Christ is the Way back." Sure enough, He is. Thank God she planted that seed! My life shows the truth from scripture: "Parents train up your children in the way they should go, when they are old, they will not depart from it" (Proverbs 22:6). I can see now that not getting caught the year I was spiraling out of control dealing drugs was an ultimate blessing.

While I was never caught for dealing drugs, nevertheless, I went to prison. It was for a crime I didn't commit. As an act of revenge, my stepfather's brother set me up, and I had to take the fall for him. He wanted revenge because my mother shot his brother. My mother was a victim of domestic violence by his brother. But she was not the kind of woman to just let it happen. The first time her husband put his hands on her, she shot him and called the police. They took her into custody, took her statement and released her for self-defense. Thank God he didn't die.

In spite of all I'd been through and seen, I prayed to God and asked him to bless me with a husband and a son. I promised that I would live my life for Him if He got me out of jail. It took four months and sixteen days, but God got me out and truly saved my soul. But the devil came in to imitate God and sent a man after me that God didn't send to me. (Be careful: every woman or man is not from God.) I was given the opportunity to be totally free from this man and not bear his seed.

I was on the operating table waiting to get a D & C because the doctor initially said the pregnancy wasn't viable. I was still growing in my faith, and while lying there, I privately prayed to God. The rolling tears falling down my face caught the eyes of the doctor, who instructed the nurse to take me for an ultrasound to double check in case I had a viable pregnancy. I was whisked away into a cold room somewhere in the hospital.

The sonographer began the ultrasound as I continued to pray. The sonogram revealed what I knew in my spirit. He said, "Ma'am, you have a viable pregnancy, and the fetus is in the right position."

I thought this would change everything. With the promise of a baby, maybe the marriage could work. But I only misled myself as the marriage became abusive. I had to literally fight him on the front porch in my panties and bra after being kicked in my pregnant belly and told how much I wasn't loved. Yet God allowed me to deliver a beautiful baby boy, eight pounds and fourteen ounces. I named him Marcus (which means "warlike") because he was born in a war for my spirit.

Then, the God in me caused the devil in him to flee. I was no longer bound.

One year after the birth of my baby boy, I developed cervical cancer. My mother did not have the same faith as me. She worried a lot. She had me dead and buried, all while asking for custody of my only son at the time. Yet I learned how to strip naked like Adam and Eve before they ate the apple, fall on my face and worship God, repeat His Word back to Him and ask Him to instruct the doctors and order my steps. (News flash: A good *woman's* steps are ordered by the Lord, too! Not that I've done anything that good, but I have repented.)

I went on to have laser surgery on my cervix. I woke up after surgery to no anesthetics in my pelvic area. I was in excruciating pain, unable to stand up or walk. The doctors told me that the cancer could come back in two months, six months—they didn't know. But God healed me of cervical cancer and stood me back upright to walk within one week.

I've been depressed, had anxiety attacks, been locked away in my own personal prison in a private hospital room, and God comforted me. In His infinite wisdom and mercy, He allowed my high school crush, Jeffrey, to come back into my life. After thinking I would be barren and that cervical cancer would never afford me the ability to have any more children, He blessed me with two more beautiful baby boys, Juwan and Javon. I often say I have one son for the Father, the Son and the Holy Spirit.

Our thoughts are not God's thoughts. I've dealt with tragedy and pain. My mother and her mother died eight hours apart on the same day. I had to close out my 401K and bury them both on the same day. (That's a note to some families: don't just prepare to live, prepare to die both for the grave and heaven.)

Guided by the Holy Spirit, I was instructed to go back to school and get my accounting degree. I started a successful accounting firm and had a long career of helping several different corporations because I relied on my faith and my rite of passage that helped me to forgive myself. Second Corinthians 5:17 states: "Therefore, if anyone is in Christ, he [she] is a new creation; old things have passed away; behold, all things become new." That scripture confirmed I was no longer bound forever. Nothing could hold me back, and the possibilities were endless. With this next-level faith, God allowed me to get my Master's degree in Accounting and Finance. I've worked for many years in this field, and numbers still run in my head. I believe because God is a God of multiplication, He's added to my life more than I deserve.

There have still been demonic attacks on my family, including a major car accident caused by a teenage drunk driver that took my passenger's life. The enemy thought he would take me out, but I've pressed on, talked it out in therapy and stayed in prayer. By divine order and answer to prayer, I requested to retire at age fifty-five. God did it three years earlier. Am I angry that I suffer from a pinched nerve with limited use of my right arm; lost an over $100,000.00 salary that could have potentially become more with my MBA; suffered nightmares; wake up with pain, and have spent countless sleepless nights as I cried out to God for the young man I had to drive to his death appointment to stop a young teenage drunk driver from drinking and driving? Of course not. At least I'm not angry with God. It has allowed me to put life in a spiritual perspective and be a light to a dark world because I have so much experience with how darkness manifests itself. I've developed a deeper personal relationship with God for over 30 years now. Not only is He my Father but my best friend. I can talk to Jesus and the Holy Spirit and know that God is listening. I will never forget the times He personally answered little ol' me.

Eleven years ago, I became a licensed evangelist. From that time to now, I've gone on to be appointed as Assistant Pastor of E-church for Trinity Temple, COGIC (that is an unprecedented feat in itself). I am humbled by and grateful for God's call on my life. Writing this book solidifies God's purpose for me to teach and preach the gospel of the Kingdom until the end comes—or at least until He calls for me.

* * *

The 50 inspirational parables that I share here are short, some-times allegorical, sometimes creatively worded, sometimes real-life spiritual stories. I also include commentary and questions for the reader. All were birthed out of everything I've gone through as well as the many conversations with God that have inspired me to live each day to the fullest. You'll never know when it will be your last day. Life is too short to allow yourself to fall by the wayside and stay. I pray these inspirational parables will bless and inspire you. I pray my testimony will unleash a wealth of faith in your life in our Father, God and that you'll trust Him like never before. May each inspirational parable bring memories to you that reveal growth through your own personal life journey and may they help grow you as a person. May they stir up thoughts in your non-ge-netic DNA that God has already embedded in you. As you draw from these inspirational parables, jot down responses in the Daily Notes Acumens, I pray you discover keen insights in your spirit that help you to meditate upon God's truth daily. He will help you make it in this life!

Grace and Peace,
Shelly Lockett

SHARPEN YOUR SWORD

1.

Jesus Is Looking For You: Turn Yourself In

What man of you, having a hundred sheep, if he loses one of them, does not leave the ninety-nine in the wilderness, and go after the one which is lost until he finds it?

Luke 15:4

Back in the old days, law enforcement officers such as sheriffs, marshals or deputies would hang *Wanted* posters on trees, in store windows, saloons and hotels to draw public attention to all types of crooks, robbers and criminals. The posters, complete with a picture of the person of interest, listed the crimes they were wanted for. The reader might be advised to approach the wanted criminal with extreme caution. If the wanted were captured, they were to be turned into the nearest marshal's office. The poster might list a reward for their capture—*dead or alive*. Some of their crimes were so bad that the law didn't afford them the opportunity to be brought in alive. The law just wanted them out of the communities so that they couldn't rob, steal or kill anymore.

The Bible records that "all have sinned and fall short of the glory of God" (Romans 3:23). Although God created us in His image, God is not like man. His ways are not our ways and His thoughts are not our thoughts. He is a forgiving and loving God. In fact, He went so far as to tell us this: "For God so loved the world that He gave His only begotten Son, that whoever believes in Him should not perish but have everlasting life" (John 3:16).

God issued a spiritual arrest warrant when you were born. Many are still on the "Most Wanted" list. Jesus is looking for you and wants you to turn yourself in. He asks the question, "What man of you, having a hundred sheep, if he loses one of them, does not leave the ninety-nine in the wilderness, and go after the one which is lost until he finds it?" (Luke 15:4). Jesus is our shepherd and our spiritual sheriff. He doesn't send out a poster with our picture on it because God has known us since before we were formed in our mother's womb. He knows the sins that we have committed, and still, He is looking for us to turn ourselves in to Him for eternal salvation and not just momentarily because it feels like the right thing to do after hearing a good gospel message.

Many make the mistake of thinking that they have done so much wrong that they have to get themselves right before coming to Jesus. This is not true. I'm a living witness of God's transforming power. Nevertheless, what if the church posted *Wanted: Alive* posters to give people the opportunity to come to Jesus for forgiveness, love and unity in the body of Christ? When they do, it brings Jesus joy. All of heaven rejoices over one lost soul. God is married to the backslider and never gives up on us. He provides an opportunity to come to Him and find rest for our souls.

Ready or not, Jesus is looking for you. Turn yourself in, the reward is heaven. Once you turn yourself in, the Holy Spirit will arrest you, then release you with no charges to be a witness. You can't abide in Him without committing your life and sharpening your sword. It helps to find a place of worship, too.

(Note to the churches across the world: when God allows us to go fishing for souls and Jesus catches them, please don't cook them.)

Daily Note Acumen—DNA Questions

Think of a time that you felt struggle in seeking the Lord Jesus. Make some notes: what issues have kept you from giving your life completely to Jesus? Explore whether or not there is still a struggle to commit your life to Jesus

Christ. Pray and ask God to help in the areas of struggle. Be determined to commit those areas to Jesus and work on the areas that need Jesus' attention by giving those areas entirely over to Him. Have you ever let someone's attitude cause you not to attend a church? Do you suffer from church hurt? Remember, the person may have hurt you, but Jesus didn't. Pray and ask God to learn to address concerns. If totally necessary, find a new, genuine place to worship.

2.

LIFE CAN BE HARD, RESIST THE TEMPTATION TO MAKE IT HARDER!

But each one is tempted when he is drawn away
by his own desires and enticed.

James 1:14

We don't have to look far to see that life can be hard. We also don't have to look too far to make life harder by the choices we make. The deciding factor will be oneself. If a person is easily enticed, has desires that open the door to regret, or makes choices that have bad consequences, their life becomes harder. Nobody can make you do anything you don't want to do. I had to learn that.

So, when it comes down to it, ask yourself: Is this decision I'm making going to make my life harder? If the answer is yes, then the choice becomes clear: resist the temptation to open the door to the thing or things that make it harder. It's never selfish to take steps to avoid things and people that will complicate your life. Sometimes, we make the mistake to believe that if we choose self, we're being selfish. The mistake comes in when we are enticed by others' selfish ambitions.

So, do yourself a favor and resist the temptation to open the door to enticement. You'll only make life harder. Consider your personal desires and choices to weigh whether they are unhealthy for your mind, body and soul. Watch for times when people insert themselves into your life and send you on a guilt trip trying to make you think you owe them your life. They won't pack any bags to travel with you, they will just leave their baggage, and you'll be left to carry the load. You'll end up struggling and tossing yourself like lost luggage on a carousel of life in a destination you didn't intend to visit. Don't make life harder for yourself if at all possible.

Daily Note Acumen—DNA Questions

Make note(s) of a time you made life hard for yourself. What was the outcome and how did God intervene? What areas of life seem the hardest? Make a list of your areas of struggle. Next to them, write, "I give this over to Jesus." Then remind yourself: Jesus will never leave you or forsake you.

3.

BAD ADVICE IS LIKE BAD BREATH: NOBODY WANTS IT

Blessed is the man who walks not in the counsel of the ungodly,
Nor stands in the path of sinners,
Nor sits in the seat of the scornful.

Psalm 1:1

Advice can be good if followed and everything that advised works out for the best. However, nobody wants bad advice. It can be as harsh to our life in the same breath, as in which it is spoken by a person who has eaten a bowl of horse manure mixed with garlic. While manure is good for fertilizing, it doesn't make for good advice. Let's face it: we wouldn't knowingly eat horse manure. So why would we take bad advice and implement it into our life to make decisions that will affect our well-being?

We should be very mindful about whom we consult for counsel in dealing with life, period. This is especially true for life situations, circumstances and the path that we choose to take to make it in life. When we see people doing things that we know we wouldn't do, that is a clear indicator that advice they would offer might not lead us in a good direction. Bad advice will lead to Sin Saloon along a dead-end road. Even at its best, it will make a person graduate from Smart Mouth College.

So, it might be a good idea to do a breath test on the person you're seeking advice from. While that won't be the best or only indicator of their reliability, it's a start. After all, it's not what goes in a man that defiles him, but what comes out. Bad advice? It will defile you.

Daily Note Acumen—DNA Questions

Make note(s) on a time you've received bad advice. What was the outcome? Most importantly, how did God intervene afterwards? What would you look for in a good adviser in the future? Pray about the times that you need advice. Ask God to send you good advisers as He orders your steps.

4.

IS IT TIME TO ABORT THE MISSION?

For they all were trying to make us afraid, saying, "Their hands will be weakened in the work, and it will not be done." Now therefore, O God, strengthen my hands.

Nehemiah 6:9

For most, the mission is to make it through this present life by finding a career and setting goals to achieve it. In addition, God wants a personal relationship with each of us. For many, having that relationship seems like mission impossible. But no matter how difficult it seems, we can't abort that mission before allowing it to completely develop, or we run the risk of only ever living in an immature state.

We are each given a great opportunity to accomplish a purpose. Every purpose requires our hands. We can't let others weaken our hands with their words. As we start out, the mission can look scary. But it will look scarier if we listen to people telling us to abort the mission—telling us God isn't real. He is very real!

If people don't know Him, their first mission should be to get to know God. We need strength for the journey. The best parts come when we ask God to strengthen our hands. What we accomplish may be the answer to someone else's prayer. If we abort the mission, especially in the early stages, it could lead to a miscarriage of a great life.

You're scheduled for greatness. Don't miss the flight by aborting your mission too soon. Don't miss the mission by never getting to know God on a personal basis.

Daily Note Acumen—DNA Questions

Make note(s) of a time that you wanted to give up. What was the outcome? How did God intervene? Determine to pray and not quit when you set goals for your life.

5.
LIFE POINTS:
ALWAYS REWARD
YOURSELF!

Therefore, do not cast away your confidence, which has great reward.

Hebrews 10:35

While this life can be very rewarding, at times, it can feel overwhelming and unrewarding. We must understand that our real reward is not on this earth. Our heavenly reward is with Jesus. While we're on this journey, God rewards us every day with benefits called new mercies—and sometimes, even children.

"Behold, children are a heritage from the LORD, the fruit of the womb is a reward" (Psalm 127:3). If we get this gift from God called children, they bless our lives tremendously and allow us to leave fruit. A tree is known by its fruit (Luke 6:44). If you've experienced this gift, no doubt you know that it goes without saying that it requires times that we have to reward ourselves early and often.

If you have not had children, know that the new mercies that we all can access every morning are confidence builders in and of themselves with their own rewards on this side. We get to build careers, live each day to the fullest and rack up life points. Unlike frequent shopper points, life points are better. They are more like milestones similar to those we experience while growing up, like graduation from high school or college that we usually reach every four years that afford us the opportunity to accomplish things and endure life until we receive the ultimate reward.

I prayed in 2013, asking God if I could see what He made in Bora Bora. By faith I started planning, saved up the money. He blessed my husband and I to go in March 2015 for our 20th anniversary. What a beautiful island. I'm praying to go to Fiji next. Nevertheless, when I FaceTimed my cousin Deidra, she jokingly told me, "Girl you are doing some Kim Kardashian stuff." I laughed and replied, "No Girl, I'm doing some God and Shelly Lockett stuff." That's what you need to do: take my name out and put yours in and do some God and you stuff.

So, reward yourself, take trips and see this world and the oceans God created. Make a bucket list of rewards and actually fulfill it.

Daily Note Acumen—DNA Questions

Make a note of the times that you've rewarded yourself. Remind yourself it's okay to do so! Have you ever travelled outside of your home city? If not, why not plan a trip? Go somewhere, take a trip of a lifetime at least once in your life. Make a bucket list and begin plans to fulfill it quarterly or yearly. Don't wait for four years to go by to make accomplishments. Go somewhere at least once in your lifetime.

6.
WITHOUT GOOD DIRECTIONS, YOU'LL STAY LOST

*In all your ways acknowledge Him,
And He shall direct your paths.*

Proverbs 3:6

There's nothing wrong with pulling over on the side of the road to get directions. The problem is who we ask. If we ask the wrong person, we could potentially stay lost. Life can be like a construction zone with a lot of moving parts that never seem to connect. If we truly want to get connected while on this life journey, the one person that we'll really need to ask for directions from is God.

I tried to do things my way so many times in my early life. Each time, thanks to the prayers that had gone before me, I was blessed enough to be rerouted by God. While a re-routing can make us feel like we've hit rock bottom, sometimes, a detour is a blessing. We can be reassured that "all things work together for good to those who love God, to those who are the called according to His purpose" (Romans 8:28).

Your first purpose in life is not to leave God out. No matter what history teaches, He is our creator, the author and finisher of our fate. He will lead us and guide us through His Holy Spirit. He will never force us to include Him and He will remove Himself where He isn't wanted. If He does, we will experience the feeling of being lost. Without good directions from Him, the feeling of being lost precedes and supersedes all other emotions. So, like my grandmother told me, "Baby if you ever lose your way, Jesus is the way back."

It's never too late to get good directions from God. It's the best way to start over so that you don't stay lost.

Daily Note Acumen—DNA Questions

Make note of a time that you needed direction for your life. Who did you ask for help? How did it work out? Compare that to a time when you asked God for direction. Remind yourself to seek God's direction first.

7.
WORK YOUR PERSONALITY

No evil can overwhelm a good person,
but the wicked have their hands full of it.

Proverbs 12:21, MSG

Most everyone has dysfunction somewhere in their bloodline that they are ashamed of or don't care to talk about. Families deal with substance abuse, conflicts with arguments, disputes and feuds. Some are even violent, with an absence of love and overly aggressive. Many who grow up with this type of dysfunction have to learn to overcome deep-rooted dysfunction and embrace responsibility for their actions. Without us even realizing it, dysfunction can shape some of who we are and how closed off we make ourselves to God and others. We might think because our family didn't care, they don't care. It's never a person's fault what family they're born into or what other family members do. We need to remember: someone else's dysfunction is not our dysfunction. We're each unique individuals with our own personalities.

The ability to draw good energy towards you (and to let that good out!) lies within your personality. Work your personality by being your best, happy self. It can take a while to learn how to separate out the inadvertently negative traits you've inherited. But I encourage you: Never let being in a dysfunctional family cause you to feel guilt, shape your thoughts, or overwhelm your inner being. Those who are wicked will try to get close to and dominate those who are good. But scripture tells us, "No evil can overwhelm a good person." Guilt is not a social norm. It's used as an evil device to misconstrue situations and consume a good person with dysfunctional behavior tendencies, depending on the type of family environment they were trained in.

It's perfectly acceptable to God to separate yourself from evil, wicked influences, whether they are family or not. If their hands are full of dysfunction, and they're ready to pour it out into your life, step away, and step into your true self because your new last name is *Christ*.

Daily Note Acumen—DNA Questions

Think of a time that you've closed yourself off and not wanted to interact with others because of being afraid of others finding out about dysfunction in your family. How did you feel? List some traits you've noticed in family members that have a negative influence on your personality, behavior or habits and write down next to it: "This is not my personality." Then, try out your new last name by inserting your first name (_____ Christ). Remind yourself you're a part of God's family.

8.
IT'S OK TO SOUND THE ALARM

And have no fellowship with the unfruitful works of darkness, but rather expose them. For it is shameful even to speak of those things which are done by them in secret.

Ephesians 5:11–12

Whistleblowing is a term used in the corporate setting. A person who sees and calls out another person or persons doing something that is illegal, dishonest and hurtful to the company is called a whistleblower. The whistleblower usually struggles with coming forth as it may cost them their career.

I've coined a phrase I call *worship-blowing*. I apply it when a person is doing something that God does not approve of, and it's hurtful to their walk with Jesus Christ and to the Body of Christ —that has to be called out. The person committing unfruitful works of darkness will struggle in their worship. This blows it for both the one who is unfruitful and the one who sees it because the relationship between them becomes strained. In that case, it's OK to sound the alarm. Worship-blowing has the potential to affect a person's soul for the better. We have to be ready to live a life that pleases God and be willing to sound the alarm—even if it's on ourselves to God.

Anyone caught in transgression should be restored in the spirit of gentleness (Galatians 6:1). Many wander from the truth, but the person who brings them back from their wandering will save their "soul from death and will cover a multitude of sins" (James 5:19–20, ESV). The thing to remember in worship-blowing issues is to go to the person who is struggling in their walk and gently reason with them. Problems come when we sound the alarm to everyone else about the person. This is the wrong approach. We have to keep watch over ourselves unless we become tempted to sin, too. We are not exempt from how we handle the situation: we are to handle it in love and genuine concern.

Daily Note Acumen—DNA Questions

Make a note of a time that you've had to sound the alarm on yourself or someone else in either whistleblowing or worship-blowing. How did it end and how did it make you feel? Did you see God intervene in the situation?

9.

I DON'T KNOW HOW TO DO IT YET, BUT I'M NOT GOING TO STOP TRYING

I can do all things through Christ who strengthens me.

Philippians 4:13

Life can be very challenging. If we don't think we have the strength or ability to do what it takes to accomplish our goals and dreams, we can feel paralyzed with fear. We have to understand that "God has not given us a spirit of fear, but of power and of love and of a sound mind" (2 Timothy 1:7).

I was helping my grandson DJ one day in his second grade virtual school. The teacher asked each student how it was going with the lesson they were working on. Did they understood what they were doing? It blessed my soul to hear one little girl respond, "I don't know how to do it yet, but I'm not going to stop trying." I think we can learn a lot from her attitude.

It's like the cliché: "Quitters never win and winners never quit." It doesn't matter if a person hasn't won yet; it matters that they haven't quit. Don't let the fact that you don't know how to do something yet stop the progress of trying.

As adults, we have to be smarter than second graders. We can let a little child lead us into being fully aware of the strengths that God has placed inside each of us. When things seem to get the hardest, we can draw from the strength that God has placed in us through Jesus that will allow us to do all things through Him.

Daily Note Acumen—DNA Questions

Think of a time of you didn't know how to do something and you wanted to quit. Make a note of what the results were after you asked God for strength. If you didn't, ask Him the next time. Journal the outcome to build your faith file, and refer back to it when you try to accomplish anything that requires more strength than you feel you have on your own.

10.
USE YOUR FILTER,
NOT YOUR FOOL

A fool vents all his feelings,
But a wise man holds them back.

Proverbs 29:11

Making coffee requires a coffee filter or else the grinds will get in the brew. If you've never tasted a cup of coffee that has coffee grinds in it, let me explain. You might not see it coming. The coffee looks like it will taste so good—especially with cream and sugar. You take a satisfying sip. It seems great. Then after a few sips, the tongue detects something gritty. It doesn't taste quite right. Upon putting the cup down, it becomes clear: coffee grounds are all around the rim. You begin to start spitting out the coffee.

Sometimes we can't detect what gets in, but we can watch what comes out. We have to learn that our mouth needs a filter. Whether in personal or business dealings, there are times we have to tell people how we feel. If a conversation gets heated, we can't let what others say to us affect our character and reactions. Once we say something in return, we will never be able to catch the words and stuff them back in our mouth. Just like the coffee grinds got pass the filter, profanity will get past the filter of our conscience and spill right out of our mouth if we're not careful. When this happens, it means our filter is busted and our fool is coming out.

Learning to use wisdom in tense situations rather than thoughtlessly venting all our feelings may take time. However, the wiser we become, the more we will learn to hold back some of our words before we speak. Thinking before speaking is usually the only and best way to communicate. We don't always know where the pause button is located in every interaction with others. The language button seems to be set to cuss on demand in high frequency when the air waves detect hostility, that danger is approaching and when our nerves are penetrated. Lashing out verbally may be natural for some who have a broken pause button and don't want to fix it. For them, cussing people out feels like it alleviates their stress or tension in situations. But it doesn't. It can sometimes give birth to irreconcilable differences.

The mind is a funny thing. No matter how we try to move past what's been said, we will always wonder if what was said, was meant. It usually was. Words hurt.

So, learn to use your filter, not your fool. Keep the fool part of the mouth in line.

Daily Note Acumen—DNA Questions

Think of a time you've used the fool part of your mouth instead of your filter in a situation. What was the outcome? Did it affect a strong relationship, perhaps cause it to lose its bond? Reflect on what you learned and what you could have done differently.

11.
KEEP THE DRIP AND DREAM ALIVE

Now faith is the substance of things hoped for,
the evidence of things not seen.

Hebrews 11:1

Your faith will move mountains, cause walls to fall and doors to open. No matter what you have gone through in life, please understand God has a purpose for every person to accomplish. It lies within you to **keep the drip and dream** alive. God's very breath contains the droplets He breathed in the very beginning that would set humanity up to succeed. Adam and Eve didn't change that; God just added more work to it. It's up to every individual to dream BIG and to keep hope alive. Your faith is the *drip*, and all that is needed is a drop to *dream*.

The disciples sought more faith from Jesus, but He told them, "If you have faith as a mustard seed, you can say to this mulberry tree, 'Be pulled up by the roots and be planted in the sea,' and it would obey you" (Luke 17:6). There will be many times when your only encouragement will come from within. Others may not see what you envision. Don't allow that to sideline your determination to succeed. Opposition should not be your focus. Leave some drip for them to draw from.

Accomplishments come from keeping it moving. Whatever your it is, don't stop pursuing your dreams. It's hard to aim at a moving target. Somebody will be successful: it might as well be you. Nothing can hold a person back except F.E.A.R.—*Forgetting Everything And Running*.

Sometimes the drip will be teardrops. If that's the case, sow in tears and reap in faith (cf. Psalm 126:5–6). God is waiting on your submission for His approval.

Daily Note Acumen—DNA Questions

What dreams do you need to resubmit to God for better implementation? How much drip is available in your mind to succeed? Make notes and write a plan of action to start today.

God Right Now, I don't know if I'm wrong But you Do, tell me if I'm wrong, please BC I don't want to displease you, So Show Me. I'll wait for your answer. I have had enough with this spirit that's running a Rampage. I'm angry and I didn't sin. God I love you with Everything In Me and I'm tired and I'm giving it to U as of Today.

Thank you Jesus And Father God!

Love your Daughter Avis R Marie Jackson

12.
DOES THIS
SITUATION
REQUIRE LOVE?

Love suffers long and is kind; love does not envy.
Love does not parade itself, is not puffed up.

1 Corinthians 13:4

It's easy to say we love somebody until a situation arises that tests the very limits of how far our love for them goes. If we had to put our love on a scale of 1–10, the reading would be on the lower end when a situation with someone tests our patience. If love *suffers long*, why do we find ourselves wondering how our patience can be so short? If love *is kind*, why do we find ourselves asking why many people are so unkind? If, we follow 1 Corinthians 13:4, the answer is LOVE will make you comply!

So many situations we deal with require love. The key to fulfilling the requirement of love in any given situation is to be kind, heed others' needs and attend to others' happiness. We're often tempted to please ourselves, and it's normal and human to think of self-preservation first. But we must remember that to preserve our reputation, we have to leave a situation better than we find it.

There should never be a time when we allow envy to manifest over our kindness. We should always celebrate another's success. As God is no respecter of persons, what He does for one, He can do for all. This same love will help us not to parade ourselves or become puffed up in various situations.

So, the first assessment we should make in any situation we face is to ask if that situation requires love. Then we can check the temperature of our heart and mind to see if we need to up our love-level. We can never give a situation too much kindness. We are required to follow the law of love. The next time a sticky situation arises and before it can get out of control, apply love. It's like a good dose of medicine. The Holy Spirit will help you determine how much love you'll need to administer.

Daily Note Acumen—DNA Questions

What situations have tested your love-level? What was the outcome, and in what ways could your love-level been increased? When was the last time a person told you, "Oh, you're too kind"? In the next situation you're faced with, explore ways to leave it better than you found it.

13.
PUT THE AIR MASK ON YOURSELF FIRST

"Save Yourself, and come down from the cross!"

Mark 15:30

In this life, we have to bear our own cross and work out our own soul's salvation. It's a daily job that requires patience and commitment. There will be highs and lows; there will be good days and bad days. There may even be days when giving up seems like a good option. Nevertheless, we have to remind ourselves, just like flight attendants remind airline passengers, "Put the air mask on yourself first." The directions are part of every flight's standard procedure before the plane takes off. Why? Because we can't save anyone until we save ourselves.

There's much to accomplish by saving ourselves first. Endurance is the key. We have to understand that we are not Jesus. While we were created in the image of God, and we can develop a further likeness to Him, would we really die for the whole world? *Maybe* we have enough love for one or two. But Jesus was mocked by the chief priests and scribes who demanded that He come down from the cross, that He save Himself. They ridiculed Him that He saved others but could not save Himself. But it was never part of the plan for Him to come down off the cross without dying first. There would have been dire consequences had He come down without first dying. Nobody would be able to gain salvation and eternal life.

Jesus' actions set the stage for all to work out their own soul's salvation. He demonstrated how we endure until the end and ultimately how we can point others in the direction to be saved. That's exactly what we do—point people in the right direction, not try to save them ourselves. We live a lifestyle that exemplifies that we're saved and we allow that salvation to speak for us.

We must never torture ourselves because someone we love is not saved. If we demonstrate our faith, they will be able to duplicate it.

Daily Note Acumen—DNA Questions

Think of a time when you've tried to save someone from themselves, from life challenges and given them the plan of salvation. What was the outcome? Did it work? Is it duplicatable? If not, what could have been done different?

14.
DON'T MIX POLITICS AND PEOPLE

For God is not the author of confusion but of peace, as in all the churches of the saints.

1 Corinthians 14:33

This should go without saying: "Don't mix politics and people." Otherwise, one just might start an insurrection.

If we want conversation to remain civil today, it seems we have to find anything other than politics to discuss. In 2021, we witnessed some people place undue faith in a man now a former president; nearly half the country held him higher than the belief to uphold the Constitution. Upholding the laws and statutes of the land should take higher priority than supporting any single person. While our right to vote should never be taken lightly, how we vote should not be left to the decision of others. The time that one could spend debating politics can be better used to read up on the Constitution to better understand the laws of the land. Many are unfamiliar with the laws of Congress and couldn't tell anyone what any amendment declares for rights. "We the people" has been reduced to a cliché. People misuse the phrase to refer only to those who believe just like they do: they twist the laws of the land to benefit only a particular race or class of people. Discussing politics can come at the cost of friendship or even kinship. At their worst, disagreements over politics have led to homicides and jail sentences.

I bring the topic up to encourage you to keep the main thing, the main thing. God is not the author of confusion. If both our eyes and our ears are open, they will never deceive us. We are capable of determining right from wrong. But I'd advise not to push your political point of view onto another. Mixing politics and people always leads to a great divide.

Daily Note Acumen—DNA Questions

What was the last political conversation you had with another person or group of people? Explore what your feelings were after the conversation ended. What could have been left unsaid? Did you say anything to brighten the other person's day?

15.
I Can't Live Your Best Life, I Have to Live My Best Life

I have been crucified with Christ; it is no longer I who live, but Christ lives in me. And the life which I now live in the flesh I live by faith in the Son of God, who loved me and gave Himself for me.

Galatians 2:20

Every day we are given on this earth is a blessing. We don't know what each day will hold until we come to the end of that day. The possibilities each morning are endless. We should seek to live our best life every day to the fullest as Jesus came not only for our personal salvation but to give us a more abundant life.

To live each day to the fullest and discover our best life—the life God desires for us—we have to delight ourselves in the Lord. As we do, He will give us the desires of our heart. To learn how to live our lives fully, we can't just copy what someone else does. It involves having a personal relationship with God, which means we have to follow God's leading on an individual basis. Just as we can't die in place of someone else, we can't live for anyone other than ourselves. Jesus Christ died for us so that we could freely choose to live through Him. To replace our flesh, to be fully committed to Jesus Christ, requires faith. When we place our faith in Him, we can live our best life as He then lives in us.

When you are fully living through Christ, your best life will shine out, because His light is in you. You will be a light in the darkness. Others will notice, and they will want your best life. Unfortunately, life doesn't work that way. We each have to live our own best lives through Christ. We can't just adopt or mimic anybody else's life. Others will see the glory but never fully know your story and what it takes you to live your best life. So, always be ready to tell the story that the best life comes through Jesus Christ.

Daily Note Acumen—DNA Questions

What does it mean to you to live your best life? What steps have you taken to live life through Jesus Christ? Make a list of the rewards on this side that you know have come from God. Now, compare that with knowing it could always be worse—other people have suffered more than you. Write down a plan of action for your day that includes some items that will make your day rewarding.

16.
THE FIRST STEP TO NEEDING COUNSELING FOR LIFE

Set your mind on things above, not on things on the earth.

Colossians 3:2

We must endeavor to protect our minds at all times. It's so important that God said, "Let this mind be in you which was also in Christ Jesus" (Philippians 2:5). I'm an advocate for mental health because mental illness is real, and I believe there is nothing wrong with seeking counseling. Some people need years of counseling due to abusive influences of others on their mind. In addition, the number of fiery darts that the enemy uses to throw at the minds of people is unfathomable.

We have the ability to overcome anything through the power of God because He created us in His image. If we hang on to another's every thought of what kind of person we should be and what actions we should take to handle life's trials, tribulations and circumstances, we will diminish our God-given ability to simply think for ourselves. We have to be careful about feeding into others' perceptions of us and our life.

The first step toward needing life-long counseling is to allow people to get on your nerves. Some people just know how to get on your nerves, pushing their way through to your reserved nerves and finally get on your last nerve. Once we know better, we can proactively protect ourselves from potentially abusive situations.

We can't put a price on peace; achieving peace of mind is like finding buried treasure. When we find it, we must protect it. God will keep us in perfect peace when we keep our minds on Him and when we trust Him with our thoughts (Isaiah 26:3). When we fully trust God and allow Him to give us His peace which surpasses all understanding, it is then that He guards our hearts and minds through Christ Jesus (Philippians 4:7).

You can learn how to renew your mind by feeding it positive food for thought. To start, consider the conversations and people we surround ourselves with on a daily basis. We have to make sure those two things aren't corrupt or deceitful. If you allow ungodly influences in, you open the door to nerve-altering ideas from all directions. Those ideas make us irritable and full of anxiety in dealing with life and people. Remember: nerves don't break down, but if we're not careful, we will.

Daily Note Acumen—DNA Questions

Think of a time that someone got on your nerves. What irritated you the most? Examine whether or not you could have done something to prevent it. List how allowing certain people access to your personal space makes you feel. Write down some things that you can do differently and practice them the next time you're dealing with someone who gets on your nerves.

17.
REMIND YOURSELF: IT'S GOING TO GET BETTER

For I know the thoughts that I think toward you, says the LORD, thoughts of peace and not of evil, to give you a future and a hope.

Jeremiah 29:11

We face many challenges. It's easy to get down and depressed when we have to go through things that we aren't prepared for, such as losing a loved one, having to take a job with modest income. We lose some things that can't be replaced. But we can't let ourselves lose who we are: we are irreplaceable regardless if someone tells us that we're replaceable.

God doesn't spend His time thinking bad things about us. He is a peaceful God. He's full of love, not evil. He has great plans to provide a future and hope for our well-being. When things are going wrong or not as we planned, our task, tough as it may seem, is to remind ourselves: **It's going to get better.**

How can we know that it's going to get better? We can encourage ourselves with God's thoughts and be reassured by what He has told us Himself. Things never stay the same. Everything changes at some point or another. What would it benefit us to discourage ourselves when God wants us to be encouraged? We can be thankful for having our health, family and faith. If we have a portion of those three and a firm foundation of trusting God's thoughts, we can see the light grow brighter as we begin to trust what God tells us in His Word. He stays up all night long to watch over His Word. We can trust His process for our life.

Daily Note Acumen—DNA Questions

Write down what you need to get better in your life. Then remind yourself to trust God and the process. Ask God to show you his plans for your future and the way to make things better. Track the outcome of each thing you wrote that needs to get better, monitor for progress and build your faith file.

18.
IT'S NOT BEYOND
YOUR REACH

You are not restricted by us, but you are restricted by your own affections.

2 Corinthians 6:12

Life doesn't require a ladder, contrary to what some people think. The world tells us something different, especially when it comes to success. We are taught we have to climb the ladder of success. But where is the ladder located? Life is as spacious and wide-open as a 10,000-square foot mansion. There is room to spread out and grow. The key is to remember that others can't restrict us.

Restrictions and barriers to success typically come from within. We can be our own worst enemies. To avoid ruining your chances at success:

1. Don't fence yourself in with negative thoughts and bad self-performance reviews.
2. Expand your thoughts and horizons.
3. Stop living in a small, cramped apartment in your mind. Get a new lease on life.

Success is not beyond your reach!

Whatever you desire to achieve, you can achieve by stretching beyond the perimeter of your mind and seeing yourself where you want to be. Just like the FDIC backs a bank, but normally only up to $250,000.00, there's a full guarantee backing your success, and it comes straight from God. To access that guarantee, you need only to: "delight yourself in the LORD, and He shall give you the desires of your heart" (Psalm 37:4).

Daily Note Acumen—DNA Questions

What was the last thing you attempted to accomplish? What goal plan did you set in place to achieve it? Did you consult with God? Make a desire list and write after each item, "It's not beyond my reach." Then, talk it over with God and write down a plan of action. Track the time it takes to achieve it, and don't give up.

19.
NEVER GET ANGRY
WITH GOD

Don't grieve God. Don't break His heart. His Holy Spirit, moving and breathing in you, is the most intimate part of your life, making you fit for himself. Don't take such a gift for granted.

Ephesians 4:30, MSG

Harsh realities can leave us searching for answers. Harsh realities like, we can never turn back the hands of time, we may not live to see tomorrow, and sometimes we can't rely on anyone but ourselves. Life isn't perfect: failure is part of the plan. However, many people don't bother to examine for themselves the answers to why bad things happen. Some don't even want to acknowledge that bad things are simply part of life. They bury their heads in the sand in denial or they find a way to blame God.

One of the major complaints people lodge against God is the loss of a loved one. Death feels so final when we're faced with enduring the rest of our journey on earth without the person that seemed to matter most. Losing a loved one is hard, but losing anything that really matters to us usually provokes us to ask, *Why?*

In response to loss, people often feel the need to vent their emotions. Extreme grief can lead to anger. This strong feeling frequently gets targeted back at God. When we see Him as the divine creator, we know He has the authority to decide who lives and who dies. And it's true: God has the authority to prevent anything.

But we must trust He is working behind the scenes on our behalf. He appoints the times for all things to transpire. We have to trust the process and know that what His Word says is true: "And we know that all things work together for good to those who love God, to those who are the called according to His purpose" (Romans 8:28). We can't get angry at God for working out His purpose. He's omniscient. There is no comparison between the hard times we experience presently from the blessed times that will come.

God holds some things we think we need or should have back for a reason. We only see His reason after the fact. Since He has infinite knowledge, authority and power, it should comfort us to know that joy and sorrow are both contagious, and they both are part of the process. We can help to infuse everyone around us with joy and we can console those in sorrow. We need to encourage ourselves and not get angry at God. No matter what we face in life, God is concerned about the things that concern us and He will never leave us or forsake us. He allows for us to be "angry and sin not" (Ephesians 4:26 KJV), but He does not want us to direct our anger towards Him. We shouldn't grieve God because it breaks His heart and because His Holy Spirit is moving and breathing in us. If we grieve as if we have no hope, we deny the hope He's given us.

We can turn to him in our pain: this is the intimacy we have with God, and it shouldn't be taken for granted. Many will curse God out because of how they feel, not realizing *He* feels for us and that there is a process to all things. Be careful: don't even curse God in a playful or acting manner. He is a Holy God. Remember, while we don't want to offend God, we might have to offend others by choosing God over them to keep from breaking God's heart towards us.

Daily Note Acumen—DNA Questions

Have you ever been angry with God? Ask yourself what were the circumstances that you believed to be God's fault. Make notes. Then examine what the underlying factors were that caused the loss or sorrow that led to anger. If necessary, write down whether it was part of the process that worked in favor for your loved one who expired or yourself in the loss that was personally experienced. Determine from your notes, if you need to apologize to God. Then trust that He is a forgiving God and forgive yourself.

20.
Everything Is Not For Sale— Neither Should We Be

Buy the truth, and do not sell it,
Also wisdom and instruction and understanding.

Proverbs 23:23

There was a time when God looked upon the earth and found that it was corrupt and that all flesh had corrupted their ways. God said that He would never put more on us than we can bear. He has made a way of escape to keep us from being corrupted. Sometimes, random life situations occur and the powers that be, like movers and shakers, bureaucrats, a frontman or frontwoman that initiate events and influence people, feel they need an escape clause other than what God's Word provides. Their reasons never embody the truth. They seek to use persuasive measures to avoid having their own personal circumstances and situations negatively impacted. By my definition, they misuse, confuse, or abuse facts and details that are relevant to bad events or actions they take against others. For example, bad actors try to justify or cover things like the slavery of a human race, the Flint, Michigan water crisis, a non-rigged election; they'll fire people for telling the truth, commit malpractice of law and medicine for personal gain, and the list could go on from there.

God tells us, "Buy the truth, and do not sell it." In essence, God requires us to get wisdom—He gives it to us if we ask. He wants us to follow His sound instruction and use good judgment. He backs up His Word by instructing us not to pervert justice; He says we should "not show partiality, nor take a bribe, for a bribe blinds the eyes of the wise and twists the words of the righteous" (Deuteronomy 16:19).

Why not take a bribe? A bribe will blind even the wisest person and undermine the intentions of people seeking to tell the truth. **Everything isn't for sale, and neither should we be.** We can't put a price on truth; nor can we put a price on our soul. We're never to sell the truth for love or money. If we allow ourselves to be bought or sold, we compromise our integrity, we start down a path of wickedness, and we begin digging a hole of deception.

There is another thing that is not for sale, and that is the gift of God, which is the Holy Spirit. Peter and John were apostles who went to Samaria and prayed that the people who received the word of God there would receive the Holy Spirit because they had only been baptized. Peter and John laid hands on them, and they received the Holy Spirit. A sorcerer named Simon saw this. In response, he offered them money because he wanted the same ability—that anyone he laid his hands on would receive the Holy Spirit. Simon's motivation was not to receive the Spirit but to get rich. But there is not enough money in the world to buy the gift of God. We must be born again by the Spirit of God, who will teach us all things and provide us the ability to distinguish between good and evil. To keep from the temptation to sell the truth, we need the Holy Spirit.

The Holy Spirit will provide us with wisdom, instruction and understanding if we ask. If we are faced with a proposition to lie, we must always choose to tell the truth. Even if we're faced with someone else who is not telling the truth, it's not polite to call the person a liar. If you're asked if a person is lying, always make sure to simply say that they're not telling the truth. Truth supports itself and should never be sold. Selling the truth, which is your integrity, is like selling your soul. When this happens, it makes you, the perpetrator, a namby-pamby person. Only the truth will make you free.

Daily Note Acumen—DNA Questions

Have you ever been entangled in a web of deceit or deception meant to keep people from discovering the truth? Do you work in an industry that deals with a deep level of confidential information concealed from public knowledge? Are you sworn to withhold information even if many lives will be affected? If so, how do you cope with that on a daily basis? Have you ever been asked to lie about anything? Did you do it? What was the outcome? Have you ever been asked to tell the truth? Did you tell the truth or not? How did it feel? Was there a sense of freedom? If not, does the incident still haunt you? Ask yourself, does the ability to be bought exist within you? If so, at what price? Then consider: is it worth your soul? Decide for yourself how important the truth is and determine never to sell it.

Have you experienced the Holy Spirit? If not, consider asking God for His Spirit.

21.
YOUR ISSUES ARE NOT MY ISSUES!

Bear one another's burdens, and so fulfill the law of Christ.

Galatians 6:2

There is a difference between issues and burdens. The first thing to remember is that other people's issues are not your issues. Issues normally require action or a decision. Rarely will such a decision require putting one person in a position to decide something for someone else—unless it's something as serious as life-or-death situation involving a ventilator. Some people make it a practice to vent their issues to another person, making the other person a part of their issues. This creates unnecessary baggage for the listener.

The Bible speaks about bearing the burdens of others. *Burdens* are different from issues. The burden of grief, dealing with a loved one's sickness or suffering are a few things we can help another person with by sharing supporting scriptures in the Bible and praying with them. If someone is always facing a financial crisis, family or marital relationship problems, workplace drama, mental confusion: these are issues that are beyond our control. We are not obligated to bear one another's issues. Burdens are borne with difficulty and out of obligation. We cannot take away the pain for others. When we understand the difference, life is much simpler. We simply don't need to carry others' unwanted issues.

Learn to distinguish between issues and burdens. There will come a time when your empathy is necessary, and through it, you will help somebody else to bear their burden. Through prayer, and without inserting your personal desires, you will show you care enough to do what can be done for them. But remember, it's fair to tell someone, "Your issues are not my issues!" The way you say it matters. Simply say, "It sounds like you have an issue that I can only support with prayer." You'll show you care, but you won't be entangled in something you shouldn't be. To bear the burdens of others, we walk humbly besides them to support them where they are in their walk with Jesus Christ. This way others learn to mind their own business, and it teaches everyone how to mind their Bible.

Daily Note Acumen—DNA Questions:

Have there been times that someone made their issues your issues? How did it feel? Were you able to help them or make a difference? Did it weigh you down or make you feel indifferent? Could a detection be made that they were experiencing a burden or an issue? Make note of a time(s) when you had your own personal issues or burdens and how God intervened.

22.
AVOID ANYTHING THAT MESSES UP YOUR SLEEP

I lay down and slept;
I awoke, for the LORD sustained me.

Psalm 3:5

Sleepless nights spent tossing and turning have multiple causes: physical circumstances and worry may both be at play. If you struggle with sleep, I encourage you to work out the situations, trials and tribulations that may be contributing to the problem. If anxiety rules your night, you can begin the healing process now.

There are physical influences we can control to help prevent sleepless nights. Eating a huge meal before bed can cause heartburn symptoms and disrupt sleep. If at all possible, we should sleep somewhere comfortable. If the room is too cold, too hot, or too noisy, those factors will mess up our sleep. A long nap during the day will disturb our night's sleep. Drinking too much before bed will cause multiple rest-disrupting trips to the restroom. Stimulants such as chocolate, coffee, cigarettes or alcohol (which, when first consumed, acts as a temporary stimulant and signals the brain to release dopamine) will keep a person awake and prone to becoming the life of the party. If consumed past the stimulant level, alcohol becomes a depressant. If the body can handle more of the stimulating affect, a higher risk for alcoholism exists. In light of this, it's another reason to avoid anything that sends the mind out of self-control.

If a person works out at night or purposely sleeps less to work more, the body will not recognize when it's actually time to sleep. Factors like these are largely in our control. We can choose to avoid these causes that mess up our sleep.

God loves us so much that He gives His beloved rest. He is our sustainer through the night, as Psalm 3:5 explains. When we lay down and get into a deep sleep, we lose consciousness of where we are. We awake by the grace and mercy of God, and we should recognize and find comfort in the fact that just as He continually watches over His word, He watches over us all night long.

Researchers at the National Sleep Foundation suggest getting between seven to nine hours of sleep. Anything less is considered sleep deprivation. Getting a good night's rest is important for our health, growth and development. We need to be free from anything that troubles or disturbs our peace and keeps us from being able to sleep.

Remember: don't let anxiety rule your night.

Daily Note Acumen—DNA Questions

Have you ever felt the peace of God when preparing to go to sleep? Do you say the Lord's Prayer before bed? This would be a great time to release your anxieties over to God and prepare to rest in Him. Make a note of habits that hinder your sleep. What items on the list can you control to improve your sleeping habits? Do you experience restlessness even without using known stimulants that cause sleepless nights? If your sleeplessness continues, it may be time to consult your physician.

23.
MOST DON'T START AND GET MAD BECAUSE THEY DON'T FINISH

Brethren, I do not count myself to have apprehended. But one thing I do, forgetting those things which are behind and reaching forward to those things which are ahead.

Philippians 3:13

Most are told to "keep their eyes on the prize" and be determined to succeed. We have to decide what prize we are going to keep our eyes on. If we don't have a prize (a goal) in mind, our eyes wander aimlessly, and our efforts will be fruitless. We can never start towards a goal with everything figured out, but to make it, we do have to start.

Sometimes, negative things from our past will hinder our progress. We may have been told we won't succeed; we may have financial burdens; we may not have the education someone else has. To succeed, we have to be self-determined. If we are determined, we will put things that don't aid our growth behind us (be it a faulty belief system or any other barriers).

If we endeavor to reach forward and just keep moving, we'll be hard to stop. We can say: "No weapon formed against [me] will prosper" (Isaiah 54:17). The enemy's arrows will be ineffective because it's hard to shoot a moving target. It's even harder if we as targets make Jesus our focal point. When Jesus is the center of our lives, He makes intercession for us. As we team with the Holy Spirit, He teaches us all things and leads and guides us toward the prize.

A prize, a goal, or a dream can quickly become no more than a wish if we do nothing to make a plan of action. We have to keep our eyes on the prize, we have to start, we have to keep moving because success does not come overnight. By staying focused and determined, we invite success in. We can extend an invitation to success by speaking it into the atmosphere. Try it: "I will start and finish."

If we don't start on our own personal goals, we will have nobody we can blame, and we can only be mad at ourselves if we don't finish. Nevertheless, past regrets of failures have a way of still wanting to take us out on a date and make us pay for the meal. There may be some things (such as mistakes we make along the way) that will try to hinder us, but we must forge ahead. We have to press forward in doing what it will take to succeed and be patient enough to track our results. Live without regrets so you can marry your success.

Daily Note Acumen—DNA Questions

Examine your life to see if there are things that you should have finished at this point that you haven't even started, or if there are directions or goals you began to make progress on that you left behind. Make a note of those items and begin a "Success" bucket completion list. Determine to finish anything that you've started and track your progress. Ask God to intervene to help you press toward the prize.

List who you're sharing your success with and consider: are those people positively or negatively affecting your goal? What can you do to change the narrative if you need to?

24.
DON'T SECOND GUESS GOD OR YOURSELF

In all your ways acknowledge Him,
And He shall direct your paths.

Proverbs 3:6

No matter what life throws at us, we have to learn to trust God in every area. This trust must come from the very bottom of our hearts and overflow into recognizing who He is. In turn, He will provide direction for our journey along every path we take and turn we make. The road to life is too broad to travel alone without God and sometimes too rocky to do it on our own. Never think that you know everything. God is the omniscient one. He has unlimited knowledge, understanding and full peripheral vision. Nothing can or will escape God. It is best to consult with Him regarding anything we desire or want to achieve.

With this level of trust in God, we can be certain He will help us. The Word reassures us: "Be anxious for nothing, but in everything by prayer and supplication, with thanksgiving, let your requests be made known to God" (Philippians 4:6). He has all the time in the world to provide direction for our life. We don't have to be afraid to tell Him anything that is going on with us. He desires to hear from us.

People miss opportunities to hear what God thinks concerning them because they spend more time talking to everyone else instead of God. Before long, seeds of doubt set in. When they do, people begin to second guess themselves and doubt God's care and direction. The seeds of doubt can give way to worry and breach the mind like water bursting through a dam. The floods of distrust cover the roads of recovery and open the gates of anxiety. Then we find ourselves wondering how to repair the breach of our mind.

Thankfully, God is a restorer because His name is at stake. He's made promises, and whether we trust Him or not, He always lives up to His Word. There's never a reason to second-guess God.

If we're rooted in God and we examine the truth, we will learn that our instincts are generally on point, and we shouldn't second guess ourselves.

Daily Note Acumen—DNA Questions

Think of a time that you should have trusted God's guidance and didn't. What was the outcome? Write down areas of your life where you need more trust in God and His Word. After each item, write, "God direct my path." Monitor those areas for change, continue to acknowledge God and make a vow to never second guess Him again. Work on not second-guessing yourself. Trust it'll come with time the more trust you place in God.

25.
Nothing in Life
Is Free But
Salvation. Most
Don't Want It.

For by grace you have been saved through faith, and that not of your-selves; it is the gift of God, not of works, lest anyone should boast.

Ephesians 2:8–9

Sometimes people want to know if their friend or their friend's friend can help them with a favor. They usually want that favor for free. In the African American community, it's called getting a *hook up*. Most trying to figure out the urban lingo misconstrue the phrase and think it refers to drugs, but drugs have nothing to do with it. If I ask you for a hook up, what I mean is "Give it to me for free." Some attribute a hook up to getting involved with an-other person—normally for a one-night stand. Then some define it as getting together with friends to hang out.

No matter how you define a hook up, nothing in life is free. It will cost somebody, whether it's the original purchaser, the person taking a chance on a one-night stand, or friends that hang out to-gether who end up wanting food or drinks. No matter what, somebody will be the one to foot the bill or pick up the tab.

However, there is a gift that is totally free that nobody can duplicate and give us. It was given by God and it's called salvation, and He leaves no room for others to boast about giving it. Although the gift is free, most don't want it. We're trained to value tangible things. If we can't touch or see it, we bypass it. But we have to stop and realize that God has a saving grace that He wants to hook us up with. He's a jealous God: He doesn't want a one-night stand. He wants to hang out with us, and when we hang out with Him, He will feed us spiritually.

There's no greater hook up than the one God can give us. He will open His good treasure to us and pour out blessings for us. His Word declares, "And the LORD will make you the head and not the tail; you shall be above only, and not be beneath, if you heed the commandments of the LORD your God, which I command you today, and are careful to observe them" (Deuteronomy 28:13). Who wouldn't want this free gift of salvation? Yet there are too many who bypass it. Don't be one that does. It will require faith and to love Him with all of your heart, mind and soul, but it's worth it. Take the spiritual *hook up!*

Daily Note Acumen—DNA Questions

Think about the different hook ups mentioned. Which have you taken? What was the cost? How did it leave you feeling emotionally or otherwise? Have you received the gift of salvation? If not, what's the drawback? If you could have God look through His good treasure and give you anything, what would it be? Determine if it's still logically possible. If so, ask God!

26.
STAYING POSITIVE
IS BETTER THAN
BEING NEGATIVE

A wholesome tongue is a tree of life,
But perverseness in it breaks the spirit.

Proverbs 15:4

If we allow the negative things some people say to penetrate our minds, those words can break our spirits. During stressful times, the mind is an open door to negativity. In fact, when the brain hears the sound of negativity, it immediately activates the fight or flight button—especially if we cannot stand dealing with negative people. In an instant, an argument can break out when those gathered together insert negativity into the conversation. When this happens, it's easy to detect who and where the negativity comes from. You can set the radar of your mind to steer clear every time those individuals come around because you know they have the potential to disturb your peace.

In times of distress or affliction, we need others' kind words, spoken aloud. Surround yourself with positive people. Positivity feeds the spirit and aids in healing. It provides necessary support to remaining confident in any situation, trial or tribulation. Some will say that nobody can be positive one hundred percent of the time. However, God said, "Whoever guards his mouth and tongue keeps his soul from troubles" (Proverbs 21:23). The key is to practice watching what you speak out of your mouth as if it had a secure gate on it. Before speaking, send the words that are about to come out up to your brain. Filter whether or not they contain any negativity. If they pass the test, then it's permissible to speak because **staying positive is better than being negative.**

Listening to people speak negativity all day is discouraging. Let's face it: Who wants to be around people who are constantly cynical, pessimistic and belligerent? If we have to talk ourselves out of negative self-talk, we shouldn't surround ourselves with more negativity. Negative attitudes can keep us from enjoying all that positive communication has to offer. If all that is planted grows leaves of negativity, there is no room for positive, wholesome fruit on your tree of life. Positive fruit helps us mature and develop the necessary coping mechanisms to handle daily life.

So, learn to speak life to yourself and others and watch the difference it makes.

Daily Note Acumen—DNA Questions

Do you encourage others who need encouragement? Examine the everyday conversations you have with others. Are they mostly positive or negative? Would you classify yourself as a positive or negative person? If negative, work on changing your communication style. When a situation arises that requires a positive outlook, document your first reaction. Practice being calm.

Challenge yourself to surround yourself with positive people. If your circle is filled with negative people, reduce your circle. Write out positive words that you would like to add to your vocabulary and practice using them. Learn new positive words and make them a part of your conversations with others.

27.
TEACH CULTURE
NOT CULT
TENDENCIES

He who [willfully] separates himself [from God and man]
seeks his own desire,
He quarrels against all sound wisdom.

Proverbs 18:1, AMP

It troubles me when I see people become part of a cult. Parents raising children may feel the distinction between cult and culture is not relevant in early childhood. But in the very first stages of a child's life, parents introduce that child to their culture. Children are always observing parents and caretakers. Their spiritual beliefs, attitudes, values, morals and customs are all on display, and children absorb it all. A positive, lifelong difference can be made when we teach children and others from the beginning about their environment and culture. It all aids in the type of person they become.

Cult awareness should be on the list of what we teach children. With all the evil forces at work around us, we can be easily influenced in the wrong direction. Learning what makes authentic, nurturing godly culture increases quality of life and the well-being for people and the communities in which they live. In the same token, we have to be careful at what spiritual table we eat from when the advertisement is made that the table is spread, and the feast of the Lord is going on. If that church or organization is under a narcissistic leader, that's a feast of the beast. It may not start out that way, but over a period of time, the teachings can become corrupt if the Bible doesn't support what that leader is saying. Know the Word of God for yourself. For the past few years, I've watched churches lose their leaders because the focus was taken off of God and placed on the leaders, exalting the leader rather than God.

In my express opinion, the difference between cult and godly culture is ideology and theology combined with biology. Cults and cult leaders base their primary belief system from ideology and godly culture is to be based on God's Word and the man or woman of God called by God to articulate the gospel.

In their thinking, cult leaders are off authentic culture. How much they are off base can be subtle or overt, just like the tactics the enemy utilizes. They have separated themselves from the true God and seek their own desires. Most cult leaders isolate themselves from the rest of society. They begin to believe in their own definition of superiority and will quarrel against sound wisdom. They're usually in an uproar against their nation and in turmoil against God. They devise vain and hopeless plots (see Psalm 2:1, AMP). Most cult leaders develop their beliefs and rituals into a social movement in direct opposition to what God's Word declares. Like wolves, they like to isolate sheep and make them vulnerable to attack. This type of movement is never associated with God.

If you are not led by the Holy Spirit, deciding to worship God under a cult leader's teaching can have horrifying effects. So, be careful and mindful when you meet charismatic leaders. Their charisma can hide a narcissistic and psychotic personality. The desire to attract followers will cause them to preach nearly anything that God's word doesn't support. As soon as God's word is violated, they cross the line.

Lines are a part of life, whether you're in them or on them. Don't cross over lines that have the outward appearance of good culture but are really cults. God would never want you to kill yourself as a cult leader might instruct. (Of course, there are subtler influences a cult can have, such as separating you from family, goals, from contact with anything outside the cult, and the excuse is normally all in the name of "God"!)

It might sound strange, but don't run from people like this. You don't want to be a target. Do back away suddenly and decisively, and never return.

Daily Note Acumen—DNA Questions

How do you define culture? Do you have set principles of spiritual beliefs, acceptable family attitudes, values, morals and customs? Examine whether God's word supports what you've been taught or what you are teaching.

Study the Word of God for yourself and explore what you're being told. If God's Word doesn't support it, leave it alone and let it go.

28.
SHARPEN YOUR SWORD

Be diligent to present yourself approved to God, a worker who does not need to be ashamed, rightly dividing the word of truth.

2 Timothy 2:15

Because there are things going on in the spirit realm that are more than you can handle on your own, this life requires that you keep your sword sharp at all times. In order to land on your feet, take all the spiritual help that's available. Study the Word of God and use additional resources like *Sharpen Your Sword* to feed your spirit man. Learn to apply the Word of God to your life, and don't take God's Word for granted. Prayer is essential and it will aid you in the battle of life. Knowing what to pray will prove to be a force field of protection around your life. Many don't know how to pray or what to say to God. He wants to hear the Lord's Prayer—it's our daily prayer Jesus gave that covers us. He will listen to our humble cry as well: our humble cry equates to our concerns.

God stays up all night long watching over His Word. When you use it in prayer, it sends a distress signal to God that His help is needed. When He hears you declare His Word, He will make haste to come and provide divine intervention. Consider the following scriptures.

God means what he says. What he says goes. His powerful Word is sharper than a surgeon's scalpel, cutting through everything,

*whether doubt or defense, laying us open to listen and obey.
Nothing and no one is impervious to God's Word. We can't get away
from it—no matter what.*

Hebrews 4:12–13, MSG

*All Scripture is given by inspiration of God, and is profitable for
doctrine, for reproof, for correction, for instruction in righteousness,
that the [people] of God may be complete, thoroughly equipped for
every good work.*

2 Timothy 3:16–17

If your sword is sharp, it will prepare you for the journey ahead
and allow you to understand the instruction you need for yourself
and to help others. This is what God desires, that those who want
to do their best match His Word with their life.

Daily Note Acumen—DNA Questions

*Develop a spiritual library you can use to aid in your study of the Bible.
Share these resources with others and develop small groups to discuss
them together. Ask God for understanding of the scriptures. Read the
passages before and after individual scriptures to get a fuller
understanding of God's Word. Build a faith file and draw from it to remind
yourself of how God has intervened in your life. Write your plan here.*

*What resources do you have already? What would you like to obtain? Who
would you like to share those resources with?*

29.
Stop Fighting the Power and Get the Power

For God has not given us a spirit of fear, but of power and love and of a sound mind.

2 Timothy 1:7

In the summer of 1989, Public Enemy, a well-known African American hip-hop group, released a single titled "Fight The Power." The song was written at the request of Spike Lee, director of 1989's film *Do The Right Thing*. Its lyrics speak to fighting the powers that be in order to get free, and they address the mental awareness necessary to claim freedom of speech and mind. The song also deals with understanding the revolutionary process for black culture in achieving racial equality.

After all I've seen throughout my lifetime, I'm of the mindset that we will not raise cultural awareness through fighting the powers that be without God. I understand *the powers that be* as any enemy force united against all people having equality of life and experiencing justice for all. In light of this, I'm able to declare that we have to **stop fighting the power and get the Power.** Real power comes from God. The Word tells us that "God has not given us a spirit of fear, but of power and love and a sound mind" (2 Timothy 1:7).

We don't have to fear the powers that be or physically fight them in revolutionary combat. I believe we need change in this world, but the answer is not physical or violent revolution. The answer is to have the same love, being of one accord. Change starts from within. There are a few things that I'm aware of as an African American woman. Our ethnicity has to stop being jealous and envious of each other. We should support each other's businesses, be about business when we start them, respect each other's right to be an entrepreneur and stop always looking for the hook up or the discount. Part of the problem in some African American communities is that they won't stop fighting and killing one another. Because too many are raised in fatherless homes, we need better programs where mature men step up to teach young men how to become better men. We need to stop the violence within our own race. Remember that the fight is against the enemy, and we must stop helping the devil.

Here's a solution I'd like to offer: organize a day for peaceful financial protests, in which as many people as possible, no matter their nationality or ethnicity, stop working—just like how the COVID-19 pandemic shut the world down. We can stop catering to the division and racial injustice that exists across the world. The entertainment and sports industries could be a powerful force to help in this dilemma. We can stand up for what's right, or like Rosa Parks, sit down for what's wrong. In the bus boycott everyone stuck together. There were even other ethnicities that took a stand until they changed the public bus system. If we hit the powers that be in their pockets, we render its politics useless. We can stop spending hard-earned money in the places that support racism or on companies that don't care and support wrongdoing, rather than waiting on their Black Friday sales.

Recruit a volunteer from every level of industry and area of the workforce, even from entertainment to sports to commit to standing together. Stop feeding resources and donations to organizations formed which do not address the real issues. We 're saying "Stay woke" but keep our eyes wide open watching violence happen, yet do nothing until we see a George Floyd incident. We've had plenty of these incidents in the African American community, but the pandemic of 2020 allowed the world to see it in real time with their own eyes.

The days of peaceful marches have been affected by the US Capitol riots on January 6, 2021. I was grateful the majority of the African American community sat that ignominious failure out and allowed the powers that be to see their faults. If only the powers that be understood that most African Americans hold too much respect for government. We expect them to do the right thing at some point. We desire change, but for too long the respect has not been reciprocated.

However, money talks, and relentlessly, most African American communities have only been concerned about themselves while spending money on selfish things that don't create change but promotes their lifestyle. Meanwhile, they watch their own people die in the streets. At the same time, I understand the logic for this complacency: our people came from nothing and to gain something gives us the inclination to reward ourselves with so much we've been deprived of. Moreover, I understand wanting a revolution. But all of the fighting only leads to more death, division and chaos. We as people, even from different ethnicities, don't take the time to get to know one another in order to love one another as God commands. We need the church to stand up and embrace all people by showing them God's love. The church needs to preach about all sin not just the sins that single people out. Tell them the truth about sin and move on to form small church groups to help people deal with their afflictions and heal.

Finally, stop separating church and state because of political reasons and the concern for the church losing its 501(c)3 status. God will provide if we trust Him. He provided the PPP loans that a lot of churches needed. I know that many churches needed it, applied for it, received it and are now praying the loan is forgiven. Most churches allow it when politicians ask to come speak to their congregations, but the pastor of the church will neither confirm nor deny if they support that particular candidate. (Talk about semantics!) We need to figure out how to connect church and state. Tell the politicians that want votes to figure that out rather than make a one-time visit and offering in the collection plate.

Nevertheless, I know prayer changes things and that African American ancestors used it and trusted God. It made a difference back then and the power of prayer now will work to make a difference and again I say, "Yes!" God will provide. The power of prayer will subdue the enemy. The enemy has tricked this generation into thinking wrong is right and right is wrong, and it's on full public display. In addition, the enemy has taught that prayer will not work. So, we need to use our Holy Spirit power and be unified in love for one another. Our minds must be like the mind of Jesus Christ. He provides the soundness of mind that God has given us. Only then can we as a nation of people begin to heal the hatred and divide that clearly exists. We need more prayer vigils before people are killed rather than after they are killed. We have to reach across to other ethnicities and invite them to God's glory and stay focused on God's purpose. When people of all nationalities, ethnicities, and racial backgrounds celebrate God and rejoice together, it will fill us with the hope that we may abound in peace by the power of the Holy Spirit.

Without the power of God, we will never be able to extinguish the fire of hatred. So, in that regard, I repeat: we have to **stop fighting the power and get the Power.** God wants us to let our "light so shine before men, that they may see [our] good works and glorify [our] Father in heaven" (Matthew 5:16). The glory of God will fight for us because the battle belongs to the Lord. We must endeavor to stand united in peace. We can't get weary in doing what's right.

Remember, God created one blood for one love. That love is God.

Daily Note Acumen—DNA Questions

Examine your heart to see if you hold any hatred in it for people who are not the same color as you are. What challenges do you personally face living in this world due to your nationality, ethnic, or racial background? Next, make a list: in what ways do you currently fight for what you believe? Ask yourself: "Is that how God wants me to fight?" If not, what can you do to be a better person? What does it look like to "love your neighbor as yourself" (Matthew 19:19)?

Endeavor to get to know someone of another race and ask them to partner with you in a team exercise to track what you have in common. Note similarities, differences, likes and dislikes. Repeat the exercise with others. As you do, you will begin to gain as many people as possible to share a common culture of one blood and one love.

30.
Your Sexual
Appetite Is Not a
Meal

Foods for the stomach and the stomach for foods, but God destroy both it and them. Now the body is not for sexual immorality but for the Lord, and the Lord for the body.

1 Corinthians 6:13

There's an old saying, "Eat to live, and don't live to eat." Our physical bodies require food to maintain life, but we don't require sex to live. **Your sexual appetite is not a meal, but your body is the temple of God.** Just because food exists doesn't give us an excuse to stuff our bodies with it. Just because sex exists doesn't give us an excuse to indulge in it without a marriage license. Stick with me—I'm getting to the point. God requires that we honor Him with our bodies.

Look at it this way: a restaurant will advertise a set price and allow people to partake in their *All you can eat* buffet. The restaurant owner realizes that most individuals will not be able to consume all of the food on the buffet by themselves, no matter how good that food looks. Customers may take more than they can eat, and say at the end, "My eyes were bigger than my stomach" after trying to eat all that tempting food!

Now, in addition to food, our natural eyes are also drawn to beautifully sculptured bodies. God has creatively blessed us with alluring physiques—breasts, buttocks, muscles—that captivate us. Truth be told, what usually gets us in trouble is that our eyes keep looking. We have both the lust of the eyes and the lust of the flesh.

However, unlike a restaurant that sets out food, we should not set our bodies out like a physical buffet for people to pay a set price (or get it for free) and indulge in all they can handle. This is sexual immorality, and it will defile our bodies as well as expose us to the risk of contracting numerous sexual diseases. Without the commitment of marriage, sex is not just skin on skin but sin on sin. It may feel good at the time, but it violates the sacredness of our own bodies. God has reserved lovemaking for a man and woman who have been joined together in holy matrimony. There is a spiritual mystery to lovemaking that God intended for just the two of them. However, some married women withhold lovemaking from their husbands on purpose. There are consequences that come with this. It will lead to some husbands cheating. While most saved men are not going to cheat, it'll force them into a relationship with their hand that a real wife can beat if she attends to his need for lovemaking. If you're married, don't deprive your spouse of lovemaking, do it on a regular basis. This works both ways, so commit to pleasing each other's sexual desires. As a woman, I know some women and men can be shy about letting their spouse know they desire to make love. Set the mood early and often so the spirit of lust doesn't set in. The need is there even if the desire is not. The enemy will send someone to meet the need if the couple doesn't address it. Don't forget to set aside time for your own personal time with God to study the Bible, too. It will give you a balance in marriage.

It can be hard to be single. I've been there. But at the same time, some women build a wish list of what they want in a man and because of it, some of the men who try to show interest make their diss list. Many of them end up alone, single and prone to sinning. They end up having sex without commitment. But why sleep with him if he didn't make the wish list? Rather, maintain self-control and give dating him a chance. In the same token, some men looking for a wife struggle to commit because there are some women who want them to come to the table with a full plate. In essence, both should bring something of value to the relationship to build upon and find true fulfillment.

If you struggle with sexual immorality, talk it over with God and ask Him to send you a husband or wife so that you're not risking your soul's salvation. Then, in marriage, you'll be free to unleash your sexual appetite with your spouse. His Word declares, "Marriage is honorable among all, and the bed undefiled; but fornicators and adulterers God will judge" (Hebrews 13:4). In light of this, God is a helper and will never put more on us than we can bear. Thank God for His saving grace and mercy because this area can truly be a struggle.

Daily Note Acumen-DNA Questions

If you're married, have you ever withheld lovemaking from your spouse? If so, how did you handle the desire for it? Do you communicate with your spouse your desire to make love? The church teaches married couples nothing about meeting each other desires. If you have questions, sit down and talk to each other. Make a habit of checking on one another's sexual needs. Discuss freely with each other what makes each of you feel satisfied. Makes mental notes and remember to actualize them. Make sure you don't leave each other sexually famished. If you're not married, evaluate whether or not your sexual appetite is under control. Are you free from sexual promiscuity? If not, ask God to intervene and take control.

If you desire to marry, ask Him for a soulmate. If you don't have a desire to marry right now, ask God for help to maintain your soul's salvation. Share your struggle with someone you can trust for encouragement and confidentiality. Develop a list of ways to counteract moments of sexual desire. If single, beware of what heavy kissing and petting can prematurely lead to when dating to find your soulmate. Remember, an ounce of prevention is worth a pound of cure.

31.
If It's Too Tough
to Talk About,
Talk to Jesus

Casting all your care upon Him, for He cares for you.

1 Peter 5:7

Everyone needs someone to talk to, but it can be hard to know who to trust. I'll never forget when my husband told me he had secrets to the grave. "What exactly does that mean?" I asked. He explained he's had people share things with him that they couldn't talk to others about. Either they didn't feel comfortable discussing the topic at all or didn't know anyone else they could trust. My husband is a quiet person; he's not one to discuss someone else's personal business. I don't think we should discuss other people's business, either, especially outside of the family. That's the way it should be in life: if a person needs someone to talk to, they should be able to trust that what they share will not be shared with others.

Most people have a best friend to confide in. But do we ever stop to think that our friend might have another friend that they confide in? All it takes to ruin trust is to tell a second friend what a different friend has shared in confidence. Unfortunately, even in the church we see all too often that not everyone can be trusted with private information.

We've all had moments in our life that seem too tough to talk about even with a best friend. Those are the times that if it's too tough to talk about, we can talk to Jesus. We can cast all our cares upon Him because He cares for us. One thing is for sure: Jesus will never put your personal business on blast. Anxiety and guilt are usually the partners in crime that drop a dime on us. The anxiety draws most people to start talking to others and throw in the line, "I'm asking for a friend." That friend is the self and self has some tough things to talk about that can't just be shared with everyone.

But don't throw away your best friend with the rest of the people. When things are too tough to talk about, Jesus is always available. He makes daily intercession for us and knows what we need before we even ask. The best thing about talking to Jesus? No appointment is necessary. He takes walk-ins. Seeing a therapist for serious issues might be helpful, too, but that may cost a little bit more. Whether it's with Jesus, a therapist or best friend, don't neglect talking it out.

Daily Note Acumen—DNA Questions

To keep your mind and spirit free of things that can trap you in loneliness or depression, don't try to hold in things that you need to talk about. What's on your mind now? Are there issues you need to share? Take a moment to think and write them down.

Find a friend to share with when you need someone to talk to. Make sure that person can be trusted. Who is that person? What makes him or her trustworthy? If you don't have a friend you trust, ask God to send one.

Some issues you face may require the help of a trained therapist. Don't hesitate to reach out if you need guidance.

Remember, always consult Jesus—especially if what you're dealing with feels too tough to talk about.

32.
HIDING NEVER WORKS

Is there any place I can go to avoid your Spirit? To be out of your sight?

Psalm 139:7, MSG

As a teenager, growing up can seem so hard. I had my fair share of struggles as a teenage girl. I think back to the challenges I had, and I recall wishing my mother was a little harder on me. There were areas she was tough on, but those didn't seem to matter to me. One time, I thought my mother should discipline my sister. What I did not know was that my sister had already said I did it. I told my mother I didn't, but she wouldn't listen. She fussed at me bad, and I remember getting very upset, picking up an orange, and throwing it at her. As I watched the orange leave my hand and land in her chest, all I could do was run. I thought, *She's going to beat the life out of me.*

I ran to an apartment building around the corner from our neighborhood. I went up to the top floor, sat in the hallway window, and just peeked out. I thought I could hide there and nobody would find me. Of course, I hadn't thought about how long I could stay in that hallway. I was hiding without food, beverages, or extra clothing, and there was no restroom. I was torturing myself. The hours passed. I thought, *It must be about 5:00 AM.* I began to cry, and I talked to myself and God.

Many things we go through make us want to run and hide. I've learned hiding never works. Even if nobody else knows where you're at, God does. There is nowhere we can go to avoid His Spirit or hide from His sight. He gives His angels charge over us. He stands ready to rescue us when we get into tough situations. We just have to cry out to Him.

I could hear Him saying, *Go home.* I had every excuse not to face the music, but I realized that hiding forever in that apartment building window wouldn't work. I pulled myself together and walked back home. When I entered the front door, my mother was waiting with open arms.

And that's how God does us. No matter what we go through in life, if we come back home to Him, He'll be there waiting with open arms.

So, always be willing to face the music. Don't hide. Face it with God knowing that He has assigned angels to assist us in times of trouble, great or small. Control your anger and never throw an orange at your parents. (I lived to talk about it. Others might not be so fortunate!)

Daily Note Acumen—DNA Questions

Have you ever felt like hiding from situations, trials or tribulations? Where was the one place you thought nobody would ever find you? If you hid, did someone locate you? What was the outcome? God knows exactly where you're at. Have you cried out to Him? If so, what was the outcome? If not, try it next time and make notes of the outcome.

33.
DEATH KNOCKS
BUT GOD CALLS

This sickness is not unto death, but for the glory of God, that the Son of God may be glorified through it.

John 11:4

There are two types of deaths we will focus on in this parable. First, there's death that knocks to test your faith. This death knocks at your door through the forms of sickness, disease or accidents. Even suicidal thoughts can knock to test your faith and cause you to give up hope. When sickness and disease knocks, your body may feel as if it's at death's door, but this death is not knocking to take your life. When this death knocks, no matter the kind of sickness or disease—whether cancer, diabetes, heart attack, car accident, suicidal thoughts, stroke, pneumonia or COVID-19—you must activate your faith because there is no cure. But God is the remedy! While many have died of all of these, there are also many who have not.

I will never forget when I didn't get the standard smiley-face postcard back in the mail after having my pap smear. I went to the doctor to find out why, and he told me that I had cervical cancer. My family was in an uproar at the news, especially my mother. They just knew that a cancer diagnosis meant death. All I knew was that God is a healer. I stretched out on my faith, lying naked before God. I cried out to Him and He healed me. Death knocked, but my faith answered.

In 1999, I went to visit my mother. She didn't answer the door. I repeatedly beat on the door before calling her apartment manager. While I was still standing there, all of a sudden, God spoke to me: "The next time you have to beat on this door, she'll be gone. When your youngest son is in first grade, I will take her." Just then, my mother opened the door.

Two years later, my grandmother became ill and was diagnosed with stomach cancer. My mother was all upset and said that she didn't know what she was going to do without her. In 2001, late one night, the Holy Spirit woke me up and drug me out of bed to my knees. He spoke into my spirit and let me know that death was encamping about my family. I would need strength for what would come next.

Two weeks later, my grandmother would take a turn for the worse. God was preparing to call my grandmother home. We had to let my mother know, but we couldn't reach her by phone. My sister and I were at dinner with my husband. I recalled my earlier conversation with God and sent my sister to mom's house to knock on the door—as if I could stop the death call.

My phone rang. It was my sister. There was no answer at our mother's door when she knocked. I told her to call the fire department. The fire department came and had to knock the door down. My mother had transitioned to her own death; it would be 8 hours later that God called my grandmother to transition to her death. I remembered thinking she led the way for my grandmother, but I recalled what she said about not being able to make it without my grandmother. This scripture came to mind: "Death and life are in the power of the tongue, And those who love it will eat its fruit" (Proverbs 18:4).

The funeral director needed a moment to pull herself together as I sat in the same chair to make arrangements for my mother, that a day before my mother sat in and made arrangements for her mother as she prepared to accept her dying. I consoled her with these words: **"Death knocks but God calls."** I reassured the director that nobody would be back tomorrow to make arrangements for me. We both laughed and were able to get things worked out. I thank God I was right.

If you're ever sick with anything, always cry out to God—it may not be your time. Always speak life and don't grieve too long. After all, there is life after death.

Daily Note Acumen—DNA Questions

Have you ever been sick and felt like you were going to die? Did you cry out to God? Have you ever had to trust God for healing for yourself or a love one? If so, write out how it felt to trust God for healing while thinking death could occur. Grief can last longer than God appoints if we allow it to. Remember, all sickness is not unto death and there is eternal life after physical death. If you are suffering from grief over a lost loved one, find a grief support group.

34.
BEING LOST IN LIFE
IS A CHOICE

The road to life is a disciplined life;
ignore correction and you're lost for good.

Proverbs 10:17, MSG

"I can't wait until I grow up!" That's a saying most teenagers have used. When you want to do whatever everyone else is doing, it's so easy to think simply growing up will make everything better. I can recall feeling that way because of a few things I wasn't allowed to do. However, as I think about it now, I was able to do most things that I asked permission to do. For my own safety and for my good, I had to ask permission.

The road of life has to include some discipline. We must be corrected at times so we can learn to make the best choices. Typically, if children are left alone to raise themselves, they will not be able to make good choices. To enhance our development and improve our life skills, we all require training. It's so important that God spoke about it in His Word: "Train up a child in the way he should go, And when he is old he will not depart from it" (Proverbs 22:6). What was God saying? Essentially, this: if parents point their children in the right direction, being lost in life becomes a choice that can be controlled. Even if children lose their way as they get older, the foundation that's been instilled in them is still there. In order to find their way, they can reflect back on that foundation. God knows that prevention is the best cure.

While a lack of discipline creates problems, no correction at all intensifies the situation. Once damage has been done, it's hard work to undo it. God is aware that there are those who will try to take advantage of children. There are child traffickers who will molest little boys and girls. The trafficker or molester likely didn't have correction in their life and went on to do what was done to them. When children stop listening to their parents and engage with those who steer them the wrong way, they become vulnerable. It's often no fault of the child. Many children who deal with these types of situations remain lost because their spirits have been broken.

I thank God that a biblical foundation was put in me at the age of four years old. As a child, I went through molestation. I lost my way for a time, but I was able to cry out to God for direction to get back on the right path in my thinking and life because I was trained that Jesus Christ is the way. It wasn't easy to recover, but I had a choice to make. I could stay lost or "let go and let God" to make the corrections that would get me back on track to a disciplined life.

It takes time, but believe every day will get better with God on your side. Don't suffer in silence. Whether you received your foundation in God as a child, or you're finding it now, cry out to Him. He'll show you the way.

Daily Note Acumen—DNA Questions

Reflect on your life and note how your upbringing contributed to who you are today. What did your parents or guardians teach you about Jesus Christ? If you did not learn about Christ as a child, how did not having a biblical foundation effect you? Do you think your life could have been better or worse growing up?

If you have children, what have you chosen to teach them about God? Can you take discipline and correction as an adult, or does it bother you? What could you do differently now to live a disciplined life? What have you had to overcome as an adult that happened to you as a child? Explore where you're at now and what you can do differently. If necessary, ask God for guidance and healing.

35.
GOD IS NOT REACTIVE, HE'S PROACTIVE

For we are His workmanship, created in Christ Jesus for good works, which God prepared beforehand that we should walk in them.

Ephesians 2:10

We serve a God that doesn't panic, and neither should we. Life will throw us curve balls, but we have to learn to throw them back. It's easy to trust God when things are going great. How we react when things are not going the way we plan is the bigger test. We convince ourselves that we can handle any trial, tribulation or situation we're faced with because we have a personal relationship with God. It's not until true trials actually come that we either respond well in faith or we enlarge the problem by overreacting. We'll know our faith by how we react: do we trust that God already has it worked out?

We have to do what people of God are supposed to do when we receive reports inconsistent with the Word of God, and that's cry out to God. We have to trust Him when we can't trace Him. When we do, we let Him know our faith is not shaken.

God stands prepared to intervene in or control any occurrence or situation, especially a negative or difficult one. He anticipated everything you'd encounter before your beginning and according to your faith. He's our creator and has been our God since the moment of our birth because He formed us in our mother's womb. We are assured of this as His Word declares: "For we are His workmanship, created in Christ Jesus for good works, which God prepared beforehand that we should walk in them" (Ephesians 2:10).

Everything is so much harder when we don't trust God. Even those that don't know Him can have the same response according to what happens. We can be guilty of being reactive when things happen, not realizing God is proactive. But that's not faith. When there is a crisis, and we don't know what to do, we have to introduce our crisis to Jesus Christ.

One thing about it: trouble doesn't last. It may seem like bad things happen to good people, but God declares, "For I consider that the sufferings of this present time are not worthy to be compared with the glory which shall be revealed in us" (Romans 8:18). God is with us in the storms of life because He is a storm chaser. If Jesus spoke to the winds and waves and caused them to cease and obey His word, how much more will He do to the personal storms in your life? He doesn't have to be reactive because He's been proactive from the beginning. His Word decrees: "The things which you learned and received and heard and saw in me, these do, and the God of peace will be with you" (Philippians 4:9).

Remember to stop, drop and pray. God will lead the way.

Daily Note Acumen—DNA Questions

What trials and tribulations have you had to face that required faith? Did you recall God's presence at the time, or did you think you were acting alone? Consider what your typical first reaction is when unfavorable things happen. Write out steps you can take to turn to God or scriptures you can remember when you face the unexpected. Determine to walk by faith and know that God is proactive. Remember: without faith, it's impossible to please God.

36.
CAN'T DRINK OR DRUG LIFE'S PROBLEMS OUT

Don't be drunk with wine, because that will ruin your life.
Instead be filled with the Holy Spirit.

Ephesians 5:18, NLT

The funniest line I've heard about drinking was in the movie *The Five Heartbeats* (1991). The character actor Eddie Kane played said: "Just 'cause I have one, two, maybe two drinks sometime, what, I'm an alcoholic now?" Having one or two drinks doesn't make a person an alcoholic, but continuing to have one or two drinks within the same timeframe over a long period of time can alter one's ability to handle alcohol and leave them dealing with alcoholism. Kane's character continued to consume alcohol and progressed to drugs. The combination of both caused him to stop showing up for his teammates and his own personal life. If you've never seen the movie, it's a good one to watch.

There are a number of reasons people drink. Some begin with drinking just for fun because being drunk makes them feel relaxed. My uncle was an alcoholic, and he always said that being drunk gave him the courage to say things he couldn't say when he was sober. Some drink because the people they hang around drink, and it's simply a social norm. Still, others—especially those underage—are encouraged to drink through peer pressure, and they may drink as a sign of rebellion. Often people drink because alcohol is an easily available way to deal with stress.

There are motivating factors that cause some to consume alcohol—one being the belief that it will allow them to forget about their problems and worries. They use alcohol as a coping mechanism. Another reason some consume is for the mind-altering enhancement of relaxation. Most use it to celebrate or fit in. Those who use drugs will always look for the next high with drugs and that can lead to a drug overdose. No matter the reason, there is no escape through drinking and doing drugs. There aren't enough drugs in the world to make you high enough to solve your problems. Nobody can ever drink or drug away their problems. When a person is sober, they will see that their problems are still there. They may have even become worse.

It never escapes my mind about the teenage drunk driver who totaled out my SUV and killed my passenger. I was left with debilitating nerve damage to my C5/C6 cervical root that I still deal with on a daily basis. Matters were made worse for all involved. The death that occurred broke hearts and left lasting heartache in different ways for each family. The 19-year-old drunk driver went to prison. I have a forgiving heart, but I knew that some punishment must be handed down by the judge. Although she didn't get the prison time that others wanted her to get, she will have to deal with the pain her actions caused by drinking and driving. My heart still goes out to Oscar's family and even to this young woman. I think about her soul salvation and wonder if she's found Jesus because I know what it's like to experience drinking as a teenager to help mask the pain that life can cause growing up.

I've experienced being drunk with alcohol and I've experienced being drunk with the Spirit of God. Trust me when I say being filled with God's Holy Spirit is greater. God sums it up like this: "Wine produces mockers; alcohol leads to brawls. Those led astray by drink cannot be wise (Proverbs 20:1, NLT). It's best not to use drugs or to drink too much as overindulgence will cheapen life and we can never drink life problems or worries out. Instead, drink the Spirit of God.

Daily Note Acumen—DNA Questions

Have you ever been drunk? If so, why did you get drunk? Do you drink on a regular basis? If so, do you drink to the point of getting drunk?

If you've created a drinking habit to cope with problems you face, what other coping mechanisms have you tired? Have you tried using drugs to mask the pain? How did they help?

Do you feel that you have or might have a drinking or drug problem? If you do, consider joining a group geared toward healing from alcoholism and drug abuse.

Have you ever experienced God's Holy Spirit? If not, ask Him to allow His Holy Spirit to fill your spirit. Consider finding a place of worship.

37.
SOMETIMES GOD SAVES THE BEST FOR LAST

Though your beginning was small, your latter days will be very great.

Job 8:7, ESV

If there's even an inkling of a thought in your head that you've come to the end of your rope, tie a knot and hang on because God is not yet done with your life. If it seems like life has thrown too many wrenches and not enough tire jacks, don't stop the repairs. If things have not gone the way that you would have had them go, don't worry. If you're not rich or in the career that you've dreamed, don't count it all lost. If you feel like throwing in the towel, take the towel and throw it back at life: let life know you're coming! Don't bend, don't bow, don't give in, don't give up, don't break. No matter your age, if you're still alive, there's always hope if you have the activity of your mind and limbs (even if they're prostheses).

God expects you to succeed. Our latter days can be greater than our former days. For that reason, we must consult with God to find the direction He wants us to go in. We don't need psychics who charge a dollar a minute when God will tell us for free. His Holy Spirit will always teach, lead and guide us if we ask. Don't let not going to the best school or not having the best family change your thinking. We have to see ourselves where we want to be in life.

The emeritus Chief Apostle Charles E. Blake of the C.O.G.I.C. always used to say, "I see you in your future, and you look much better than you do right now." I've been under the mindset that God sees us in our future, and we look much better than we might right now.

When I was a little girl, I liked to play the game of jacks. We would scatter the jacks, toss the little ball into the air, pick up a jack, let the ball bounce once and catch it. We had to start with our ones. We couldn't get to the tens until we had successfully picked up the ones through the nines. If we fouled, it was the next player's turn. What I liked most about the game was that when we threw the jacks out to scatter them, if they came out still touching, we got do-overs.

This is the kind of God we have access to. If your life comes out scattered, don't worry. He is the God of a second chance and then another chance. We can ask God for do-overs. When we start out, we shouldn't despise how small that start is in the beginning because sometimes God saves the best for last. Like in the game of jacks, you might have to start over.

So, don't be afraid to begin again. We can't lose with the true and living God we choose.

Daily Note Acumen—DNA Questions

Examine where you're at in life. Are you satisfied? Have you fulfilled your hopes and dreams? If not, why? Assess whether you need to start over. Ask for God's help.

What are some goals you have? Write them out and test each one using the guidelines defined as the five SMART goals: are they Specific, Measurable, Achievable, Realistic and Timely?

Pray and encourage yourself. Dream big or dream bigger. Remain positive and monitor your progress.

38.
TRUTH IS LIKE A MOUNTAIN: IT CAN'T BE HIDDEN

And you shall know the truth, and the truth shall make you free.

John 8:32

We live in a world where some people are so dishonest that we have to fact check, lie detect and double check most everything that some people say. It's amazing how many are quick to believe a lie rather than the truth. Some people are purposely deceitful, lie, and think that nobody will ever find out.

However, what is done in the dark will always come to the light, no matter how long it takes. God's word declares: "A false witness will not go unpunished, And he who speaks lies will not escape" (Proverbs 19:5). God wants His people to be honest and always tell the truth, no matter how hard and no matter what the consequences or outcome will be. In fact, a lying tongue is one of the seven things that God hates. God is a Spirit, and those who worship Him must worship Him in spirit and truth. In Proverbs, we learn He hates "A false witness who speaks lies, And one who sows discord among brethren" (6:19).

Lies are derived from Satan, who is the father of lies. The truth gets its origin from Jesus, who is the way, the truth and the life. Jesus is the absolute reason why truth is like a mountain that can't be hidden. Jesus, being the truth, was hung on a cross and buried for the sins of the world. Three days later, He rose again with all power in His hands. If we abide in Him, He abides in us, and our conscience will always convict us to tell the truth.

I can still recall being in prison in Louisville, Kentucky, waiting to get out of there. I remember it wasn't like a jail but more like an old, bad, college campus dorm. If the inmates did something wrong, they would have to go before the warden and there was a jail onsite they would be locked up in. To pass the time, I worked in the paint shop. One day, a supervisor from the construction area came over and asked the paint shop supervisor if he could get some inmates to come over and lift bricks. At the time, I was standing there with another inmate, and I simply said, "I'm not going to be able to help with that." I weighed 150 pounds soaking wet. Nevertheless, the other inmate started to cuss and swear, saying how she wasn't going to do it. Remember, unless an inmate did something wrong, they weren't in jail but in a dorm. Well, about 30 minutes went by and the paint shop supervisor, Mr. Diggs, got a call to send over the two inmates who cussed out the construction supervisor. My name was given as one of the people. Growing up, I was always known as a fighter, but never a person to cuss or swear. I was delivered from punching people out, not cussing people out.

I went on to the warden's office with the other young lady. She had to go in first. After about 15 minutes she came out with a mean mug and the guard standing there was instructed to arrest her. I was beckoned to come into the warden's office. He began to tell me how the construction supervisor said I cussed him out. I could feel my grandmother, Mama Hollinshed's presence, as I sat in that seat. I recalled her telling me, "Baby, you shall know the truth and the truth will make you free."

After he finished, I told the warden that the construction supervisor was not telling the truth.

He said, "So what you're saying is he's lying?"

I said, "No sir. He's not telling the truth."

The warden said, "Why would the man lie on you?"

I repeated again, "No, sir. He's not telling the truth."

The warden said, "So you're telling me that he lied on you."

For the third time, I simply replied, "No, sir. I'm telling you that he's not telling the truth."

Finally the warden said, "Go back to your job site and if I have any further questions, I'll call you back up. If I do, you'll be locked up."

I went back to the paint shop and never received a call to return. I stood on the truth of what I was taught, to never call a person a liar. And the truth made me free for that moment. I reflected on how I was raised, with the Word of God being instilled in me and how I should have listened to everything I was taught. I would have been totally free had I listened to the truth in all my decision making, especially not hanging out with the wrong people in life.

The truth will always prevail even if someone lies about you. Don't seek revenge for yourself. When deceit is involved, the truth may take years to come to light, but we can trust and believe that it will not remain a mystery. Don't worry when people don't tell the truth and prefer to lie, especially when it's a family member that lies on you or to you. Know that just like when a driver approaches a stop sign, the driver must stop, so a person who does not tell the truth will eventually have to stop lying and tell the truth.

Daily Note Acumen—DNA Questions

Have you ever had a loved one tell lies on you or lie to you? What about someone else or a close friend? How did it make you feel? How did it affect the relationship you share with them?

Have you forgiven the person that lied on you? Has the truth been discovered? If the truth hasn't been revealed, have you prayed and ask God to reveal the truth?

SHELLY LOCKETT

39.
LIVE EACH DAY
WITH GOD'S
APPROVAL

Do not boast about tomorrow,
for you do not know what a day may bring.

Proverbs 27:1, ESV

There's an old saying: "Don't put off tomorrow what you can do today." That's a good saying, and there's a good reason why we can live by it. Tomorrow is not promised. We make many plans for the future, but often we leave God out. Most times, it's unintentional. We don't even realize that we're doing it.

We get in planning mode and it just happens. While it's great to have plans for tomorrow and not just wing it, in planning my life, I've learned that God wants to be involved. Some may ask how God can be involved in the planning process. Surely, He's busy and has plenty of other things to do. That is true, but there's a disconnect. It's not that He doesn't have time. Time belongs to Him! It's that we don't know what tomorrow holds.

We have yet to be invited to tomorrow by God. He sends those invitations out daily because He wants us to live each day to the fullest, like it matters, and with His express approval. It's not as hard as one may think to gain His approval. We must simply take the example that He has given us. His Word declares: "You ought to say, 'If the Lord wills, we will live and we will do this or that'"

(James 4:15, AMP). That's how we include God in the planning stages of life and at the same time get God's approval, if He is willing. We don't want to get in a hurry and get ahead of God.

He's given me many opportunities when I've included Him in my plans. I've watched how things turned out better by including Him rather than leaving Him out. What a difference God's approval makes and getting our Father's permission to plan is totally in order!

Daily Note Acumen—DNA Questions

Have you ever planned something and didn't include God? Reflect on how it turned out. Did it turn out great or were you all over the place in your planning and execution? Compare the difference in times that you didn't include God versus the times that you did. Try including God in everything that you plan.

Remember, whenever you say you're going to do something, say, "God willing!" first. It makes God smile. Like a good parent, He'll be available to give His help and approval.

40.
WHEN WISDOM CALLS, ANSWER!

The fear of the Lord is the beginning of knowledge,
But fools despise wisdom and instruction.

Proverbs 1:7

We've all heard it said that common sense is not common. We could also say not having wisdom is not wise. We need to be able to distinguish between right and wrong and have unbiased judgment while maintaining compassion. True wisdom is given by God.

In the Bible, God gave Solomon wisdom and deemed him the wisest man of his time. When Solomon spoke, kings from all nations would come to hear his wisdom. Solomon spoke proverbs and wrote songs that caused men and women in Egypt to tell of his wisdom to others. God passed the authority to build His temple to Solomon instead of his father David. Solomon had wisdom from God to become a master builder. Two women came to Solomon when one of their babies died. The woman whose baby had died lied to try to claim the baby that was still living as her own. Through an amazing display of wisdom, Solomon easily determined who the baby belonged to (see 1 Kings 3:16–28).

In the everyday world, it takes years of experience to gain such wisdom. However, God said that we can ask Him for wisdom, and He will give it liberally. We need wisdom to discern what is true to gain lasting insight. If we look back over our lives, we can be honest with ourselves—we haven't always made the wisest decisions. In our younger years, we probably would have done things differently if we'd asked for more wisdom at the time. That's probably why God said, "fools despise wisdom and instruction."

I will never forget the time when I was in 10th grade and one of my teachers announced to the class that we were going to take a test. The teacher specifically directed us to read the instructions first and then begin the test. I read all of the instructions and put my pencil down. I looked around and several students were already working on the test. But the instructions had said: "When you finish reading this, put your pencil down and do nothing. You're finished." It was obvious: many either didn't read or didn't pay full attention to the instructions.

That's the same way it is in life. We can read and assume we know many things, but unless we've asked God for wisdom, we'll risk failing the test.

Daily Note Acumen—DNA Questions

Think of a time that you didn't use wisdom. How did that affect your situation?

When was the last time you asked God for wisdom? Do you believe you could have made wiser decisions if you'd asked God beforehand?

Reflect on times you used wisdom and times that you didn't. Compare the difference.

Take a moment and ask God for wisdom now. Pray to know the difference.

41.
RESPECT IS NOT
JUST FOR YOU

Respect everyone, and love the family of believers.
Fear God, and respect the king.

1 Peter 2:17, NLT

Respect is not just earned but given! From the time we're very young most of us have been taught that: usually our parents and teachers start this foundation of respect. Our history teachers teach us about government and the respect that is allotted to the three legislative branches. If we were raised in church, it's followed by learning to respect our pastors, and we grow up to include our supervisors on our jobs. Simply put, God wants us to be good citizens during our time here on earth. We are to respect these authorities as they are responsible for teaching us, leading us and for keeping order and peace. When we are respectful, we are aligned with God's will, and we distance ourselves from negative reproach or consequences that the Bible alludes to when it says that those who display disrespect are fools and ignorant. We are not to break the rules. Instead, we are to break the worldly cycles of life through God's Word and show respect. Those cycles of life come in four stages: when we're first introduced to the world, our growth, maturity and eventually our old age decline. Our levels of respect normally change with each stage.

We're required to treat people with dignity and respect. We should respect and love our spiritual family. We are to respect and revere God and respect "the king" as it says in 1 Peter, which for us today is the government. When it comes to God, we usually believe that it's easy to respect Him. Trouble kicks in when we're required to respect governmental authority we may disagree with, as well as respect some in the body of Christ who don't do the same. For this reason, many people believe that respect must be earned, not just given.

But this is not what God said: He said to pray for those that persecute us (Matthew 5:44). We're required to follow the golden rule, to do unto others as we would have them do unto us Luke 6:31, Matthew 7:12). But when things go awry, those rules seem to go straight out the window.

A rapper by the name of Birdman was on a radio talk show in 2016. He felt the host wasn't going to give him the respect he thought he deserved over the airwaves. Birdman showed up for the interview, stopped the host in his tracks before he even started, and told him, "Put some respek on my name." *Respek* is the slang word for respect. Respect is a necessary component in any relationship. Aretha Franklin made that clear in her hit single "Respect" in 1967. The lyric "All I'm asking is for a little respect when you come home" moved the masses to ask for respect. The song became an anthem for civil rights and feminism.

Respect is not just for one but for all. It doesn't need to be earned; we just need to give it. When we begin with respect, we can make progress in communication and negotiations.

Daily Note Acumen—DNA Questions

What do you believe about respect? Is it earned or given? Have you ever felt disrespected? How did you handle it? Think of some methods to show respect to others even if they are disrespectful toward you. Make a note to use them in times you feel disrespected. Practice talking to others the same way you would speak to God. Remember God is watching; we want to respect Him.

42.
"I Didn't Know" Is Not an Excuse to Make It Into Heaven

"Repent, for the kingdom of heaven is at hand!"

Matthew 3:2

People use excuses to get out of situations or to keep from doing what they know they should do. It's hard to tell a person who is doing something God doesn't approve of that what they're doing is wrong. Most times, the person in the wrong will respond with an offended: "You're judging me."

I've been intrigued with a new fad I see people using to keep from committing to a lifestyle that pleases God and paves the way for them to enter into heaven. The new excuse? "I didn't know." I've heard people ask, "If a person doesn't read the Bible, how could they know if what they did was right or wrong?" God not only gave us His Word as a predetermining factor of right vs. wrong, but He also backed it up when He gave us a conscience. Our conscience is that inner feeling or voice that leads us to know whether we are right or wrong in our behavior. Once Adam and Eve ate from the tree of knowledge of good and evil, our conscience was activated. Our conscience is preset to inform us of values and principles. Even if a child is not trained well by their caregivers, they see others' actions when they are older. If they end up doing something wrong, they're instructed to do what is right. We learn from our mistakes.

Several types of conscience have been defined, including antecedent, consequent, right or true, certain, doubtful, false or erroneous, tender, lax or weak, perplexed and scrupulous conscience. Let's focus here on the effects that false or erroneous conscience can have. In erroneous conscience, the mind wrongly judges that something unlawful is, in fact, lawful. By relying on false principles or beliefs, the erroneous conscience darkens the mind and confuses the reasoning process. This gives the mind justification for carrying out things that we know or believe are totally wrong. If we allow a lax conscience, we stop caring about others or about truth or goodness. That lax conscience can aid the erroneous conscience because it tells the mind to focus on insufficient information. This lets it decide a sinful act is permissible and that something severely wrong is not serious.

The Word of God has been preached all across the globe, and there is no excuse sufficient to continue in sin and think that God's grace will abound. God sums it up when He says that obedience is better than sacrifice (1 Samuel 15:22). Therefore, we must repent, for the Kingdom of heaven is at hand. Wouldn't you rather err on the side of right rather than the side of wrong? We must teach the conscience the will of God and not that of oneself.

Daily Note Acumen—DNA Questions

Research the different types of conscience mentioned above. Make a note of ones you've experienced. Consider whether God wants people to continue in sin. If you're not saved, decide if you're comfortable with making excuses and waiting to come before God to decide your fate. Think about whether you want to be obedient rather than just sacrifice your soul's salvation.

If you're in a personal relationship with God, are you allowing the Holy Spirit to lead and guide you? Do you ask the Holy Spirit for understanding when you're studying the scriptures? Have you read the entire Bible before? If not, find a yearlong devotional that will allow you to read the entire Bible. If you have read the entire Bible, start over and read it again.

43.
EVERYBODY WILL
NOT CELEBRATE
YOU

Humble yourselves before the Lord, and he will lift you up in honor.

James 4:10, NLT

When the camera's rolling and the spotlight is on you, there will be those who celebrate with you. However, some will be filled with an evil twin's envy and jealousy, and they will not celebrate you as you rise to new heights. A level of evil comes through envy and jealousy and it's designed to stop your progress. Some people will celebrate your demise before they celebrate your rise. "The key will be to not let evil conquer you, but conquer evil by doing good" (Romans 12:21, NLT). Like David in the Bible, we will have to encourage ourselves to keep from being consumed by what envy and jealousy will try to do to us. It is imperative to know that we have the force field of God's protection and care surrounding our very being.

God wants to celebrate our success. He is faithful and prepared to establish us and guard us against all manner of evil. Remind yourself that common sense and success belong to God's people. As a reminder of His unfailing love for us, God gives us insight and strength. We should be aware, though, that sometimes the setback will come before the setup.

I'm reminded of Joseph who was destined for greatness but ended up in a pit. His brothers were so jealous and envious, they threw him in a pit. They didn't stop there: they sold him into slavery. Later, Potiphar bought Joseph from the Ishmaelites. You would think that was the end of the story for Joseph. What good could come for him? However, Joseph found an opportunity to overcome the evil done to him.

Nothing could stop Joseph's destiny because God already promised him success. God was still with him and He made everything in Joseph's hands prosper. Joseph became the overseer, and nothing was held back from him except Potiphar's wife. That didn't stop Potiphar's wife from coming after Joseph. When he refused her advances, she lied on him, and he was put in jail. This set up Joseph to meet the butler and the baker, whose dreams he interpreted. It would take two additional years for Joseph to be remembered by the butler after the butler was released.

After Pharaoh had a dream that no one could interpret, the butler remembered how Joseph interpreted his own dream. There was nobody capable of interpreting Pharaoh's dream except Joseph. Pharaoh was so impressed with Joseph's interpretation that he appointed Joseph over all of his house and all of Egypt.

The story of Joseph is unique, but it serves as a good reminder: "If God be for us, who can be against us?" (Romans 8:31, KJV). It shows, too, how we can go from setback to setup. Joseph didn't have many celebrating him, but he didn't let that stop him. He was able to conquer evil because he remembered that God celebrated him.

Don't forget God's promises for your life. It's the key to knowing your spiritual net worth because **everybody will not celebrate you.** God will!

Daily Note Acumen—DNA Questions

Have you ever had to overcome something others have tried to do to you? Journal about a time you had to conquer evil. Make a note of both the setbacks and the setups that you dealt with.

Did you seek God in spite of what the circumstances looked like? Have you ever let anyone's jealousy or envy stop your progress? How do you handle success? How do you handle setbacks? Compare the two and make notes for yourself to handle setbacks better in the future. Remind yourself: God wants to celebrate you!

44.
IT'S A GREAT DAY
TO BE GREAT!

And so find favor and high esteem in the sight of God and man.

Proverbs 3:4

I've had plenty of conversations with God. One conversation with Him was very humorous— I wanted to know who becomes great and how they become successful. I didn't start out with a blunt question to God like, "How is it determined who becomes what people consider great in life?" I was standing in front of the bathroom mirror, and I mentioned to God that most people that go on to become great or successful in life seem to have perfect teeth. I jokingly admitted to God that I believed I was just mediocre—an original of His, but humbly moderate.

For years, I had a gap in my front teeth. Although I could have chosen to do something about it when I was younger, I just never did. After that conversation with God, out of the blue, my husband began to start going to the dentist frequently. When I asked why, he said he wanted to preserve his teeth so that he wouldn't need dentures in his old age. That same week, I developed a toothache and had to go to the dentist.

As I sat in the chair getting my tooth cared for, I reflected back on the conversation I had with God, and I decided to mention to the dentist about my gap. In an instant, he said, "I can fix that." Within an hour after first completing the work I needed to fix my toothache, he handed me a mirror. I couldn't believe my eyes. Instantly, my gap was gone.

The following week, I had a meeting to attend. After I finished speaking at the meeting, the church's executive secretary sitting next to me commented, "You have perfect teeth." I smiled and said, "Thank you." When I got into my car, I couldn't help but laugh and tell God how great He is! God let me know that He has predetermined for everyone to be great, but the choice is theirs. It's not in the teeth, but keeping them up can help with personal satisfaction.

It was then that I had an overwhelming desire to go back to school to get my master's degree. God confirmed my desire at Wednesday night Bible study when my Pastor taught us this: "He said somebody is going to be great; it might as well be you. Somebody is going to make a million dollars; it might as well be you."

I thought, "It's a great day to be great. What's holding me back? There's no excuse. My teeth look great."

So, go on and match your teeth (or whatever you have that gives you confidence)! Strive to earn a good reputation and live well in God's eyes and the eyes of the people. That is what God considers being great. Don't allow anything to keep you from being what God has predetermined for you to be. God has given us access to everything we need to be great as He is the great *I Am*.

Daily Note Acumen—DNA Questions

How would you rate your self-esteem? Are you satisfied with the direction your life has taken? Do you talk to God on a regular basis? If not, have conversations with God daily—no matter how random they seem—concerning your hopes and dreams. Listen for His response and make notes.

How do you define being great? Do you only see being a celebrity as being great? If so, consider how God defines greatness. Then, prepare to be great.

45.
GET OUT OF D.E.B.T.

Owe no one anything except to love one another,
for he who loves another has fulfilled the law.

Romans 13:8

Some live in poverty, while others put themselves in debt trying to live the dream life. Oftentimes, they not only spend their money on living the dream, but they spend it trying to figure out how to become rich. From investing in stocks and bonds, planning out residual income plans, buying cryptocurrency and lottery tickets, there are endless ways to seek to become rich. Focusing on all those possibilities can be complicated. God simply asks us to "seek first the kingdom of God and His righteousness, and all these things will be added to you" (Matthew 6:33).

It can be hard to accept this prerequisite from God. A luxurious lifestyle that immediately fills the "I want it now" mindset can be very alluring. And perhaps this is understandable, for we were created in God's image. God is very detailed about how He likes things to look and be built. The streets of heaven are paved with gold. We have an inclination to like nice things. We're a chip off His block. But what makes us different, perhaps, is in how we were raised or where we grew up. Jesus said the poor will always be with us (John 12:8). Who gets grouped into that category? It all depends upon who was dealt the initial hand of poverty and whether they find a way to escape it. There are countless stories of those who did find a way.

Why would God say to owe no man anything but love and not provide a way to do it? Give God something to work with. "Faith without works is dead" (James 2:20). He has provided a way, and the main key is to prioritize God. He said, "Eye has not seen, nor ear heard, Nor have entered into the heart of man the things which God has prepared for those who love Him" (1 Corinthians 2:9). Jesus seconds that motion when He says, "I have come that they may have life, and that they may have it more abundantly" (John 10:10). That's what I call the Jesus Plan. It consists of seeking God first and asking Him to put us on the Jesus Plan to owe no man anything but love.

Next, we have to learn to **get out of D.E.B.T**: *Doing Everything But Tithing.* There are times we give to ourselves first and possibly give God a little part of what's left. I was so glad God dealt with me in this area early in my young adult life. I realized we can't beat God's giving. Will there be times we struggle? Yes— but we don't have to let tough times remain a struggle. Every day will not be a Ruth's Chris day. Unless you've achieved that level of financial success, you must monitor your finances in order to gain any level of financial freedom.

Remember to put God first, give to others in need, donate to charities and remember to tithe to a church. (Although there are those who certainly live in excess, every man of God over a church is not robbing the church or God: if you're worried about where your tithe is going, join and attend the business meeting to find out.)

Lastly, know that God will not give it to you if He can't get it through you. That simply means if you only have selfish ambitions, you might as well "forget about it," as the old Italian saying goes. You're blessed when you can be a blessing. Besides, we will take nothing with us when we die. You'll never see a U-Haul truck behind a hearse.

Daily Note Acumen—DNA Questions

Are you in financial debt? Whether you're wealthy or not, determine and maintain a budget. Map out a plan with a financial advisor if you're not savvy with money. Do you give to charities? If not, consider giving to several. Are you doing everything but tithing? If you're not tithing, start and then monitor the difference over time from when you were not. Ask God to put you on the Jesus plan.

46.
GOD HAS
A MASTER CLASS

*The LORD says, "I will guide you along the best pathway for your life.
I will advise you and watch over you."*

Psalm 32:8, NLT

Many might have first heard of the phrase master class when Oprah said it and produced a show with *Master Class* as the title. The first time I heard the phrase was when God spoke to me and ordained me as a teacher.

On a Saturday afternoon, I decided to take a walk. When I got to the park, I needed to sit down and take a break. There was a bench in the park, but I was hesitant to use it because an older gentleman was already sitting there. God moved on my heart that it was fine, and I should go ahead and sit down.

I sat down and the man spoke to me. I was cordial and spoke back.

He asked me, "How is your day going?"

I replied, "I was just getting a little walk in before I need to get back home and get ready for church."

He said, "I don't go to church anymore."

I was surprised because he was an older man. I always assume, "With age comes wisdom." Surely, I thought, he must know having a relationship with God is important. Before I knew it, that's exactly what I said.

He told me, "A person doesn't have to go to church to have a relationship and serve God."

I shared with him how God has said that we should not forsake the assembling of ourselves together, which means God requires us to go to church.

He replied, "Tell me where that's found in the Bible."

I said, "Hebrews. The tenth chapter and the twenty-fifth verse."

Just then, as if the sky opened up, I heard the voice of God say, "Study My Word. There will be many more that you will have to teach."

I was only twenty-four years old at the time. *How would that all happen?* I wondered.

It was as if time stood still, and God said, "The Holy Spirit will teach you."

The Bible declares: "For the Holy Spirit will teach you in that very hour what you ought to say" (Luke 12:12). God has a master class, and He will teach us His Word through His Holy Spirit. Many times people will not read the Bible because they say they don't understand it. And much of the church of today is almost doing away with Sunday School and Bible study. However, because I've experienced it, I know that we can learn God's Word if we ask Him for His Holy Spirit. We can receive the anointing from Him to know how to properly apply His Word to our life to live with blessed assurance, grace and mercy.

And we just may be able to teach someone else in the process. That's what disciples do—make other disciples. However, disciples must first attend the Master's master class.

Daily Note Acumen—DNA Questions

Do you find it hard to study the Bible? If so, do you ask God as you study to reveal the meaning of scriptures to you? Do you study the Bible often? If not, why? Consider that spending time in the Bible is the equivalent of talking to God. Make some time to study God's Word daily. Everyone, no matter how busy, can take the time to get a scripture in daily. Ask God for

His Holy Spirit. When you receive Him, He will guide you through the Master's master class for you.

47.
THERE'S A SOUND THAT MOVES GOD, BUT IT'S NOT COMPLAINING

Do all things without complaining and disputing.

Philippians 2:14

This life was not initially built on problems. God's original design was to put us on easy street where we'd live in responsive obedience. He gave clear instructions to Adam before He blessed him with Eve. Adam and Eve had it made: they were naked and not ashamed in their own tropical paradise. Then the original complainer brought to their attention the tree of knowledge of good and evil. In the very first dispute, Eve lodged a complaint against God by deceptively interpreting His command. In hindsight, I think if Adam had been obedient and not so smitten with Eve to just follow along, God might have punished Eve and gave Adam a new wife. That's just a solution I humorously give for Adam.

Most of us know from experience that once a complaint has been issued, it must be addressed. We can thank God that He was the Customer Service Director and had a plan of action that ultimately saved the day for all of us. He escorted Adam and Eve out of the garden of Eden and took no more complaints from them. People don't even seem to need a reason to complain. They can be on easy street and still find a way to complain about everything and nothing. Sometimes, all it takes is for one to complain, and then the one becomes two.

That tendency to join in complaining is one reason this crooked and perverse world criticizes the church so much. Some in the church itself are chief complainers: they're judgmental and do not follow the instructions that God has laid out in His Word. As time goes on, more people complain more and more every day, and all their complaining does nothing to move God.

There is a sound that moves God, but it's not complaining. God tells us to rejoice and be glad by doing "everything without complaining and arguing" (Philippians 2:14, NLT). The big picture is that we are to be bright, shining lights on display for God by showing our gratefulness for being alive and following the instructions in the Bible. "Rejoice in the Lord always. Again I will say, rejoice!" (Philippians 4:4). Rejoicing while keeping the faith will move God to act on our behalf. He has the power to change things, but we can't enter into the inner courts with complaints.

Daily Note Acumen—DNA Questions

Have you ever found yourself complaining to God? Try to change the narrative when you catch yourself complaining. Be mindful of how you approach the throne of grace to obtain mercy from God. Make a list of things that you would like to change about yourself. If complaining is one, ask God to remove the tendency to complain.

Practice rejoicing when trials and tribulations come. When we rejoice, we confuse the chief complainer, and we expedite our trials and tribulations before God. Write out this scripture: "Many are the afflictions of the righteous, but the Lord delivers [us] out of them all." Then write next to it, "I will no longer complain but pray."

48.
BEING A CHRISTIAN
DOESN'T MEAN
BEING A DOORMAT

Speak up for those who cannot speak for themselves; ensure justice for those being crushed.

Proverbs 31:8, NLT

As a little girl, I was taught to live my life for Jesus. We had to go to church on Sundays. My paternal grandmother, Alice Hollinshed, whom we affectionately referred to as Mama Hollinshed, made my aunts get up for church. One night they had been out late partying, and Mama Hollinshed came in and yelled: "If you stay up late with the devil, you better get up early for the Lord Jesus." That was the first example I witnessed of a Christian not being a doormat. She could have allowed her young adult children to run all over her by letting them do what they wanted, but she was a strong woman of God, and they were in her house. My aunts were tired, but they jumped out of their beds and began to get ready for church. When we got to church, they were attentive: they wouldn't dare fall asleep in church.

Nowadays, some people allow their children, whether they're still small or in the young adult stage, to do all types of things, talk to them in any way with no remorse. They teach no discipline. Many Christians believe that we have to turn the other cheek and allow people to walk all over us, as if this is some

Christian code set up by God under a "do unto others as you'd have them do unto you" statute. The Bible does say, "Beloved, do not avenge yourselves, but rather give place to wrath; for it is written, 'Vengeance is Mine, I will repay,' says the Lord" (Romans 12:19). This passage of scripture doesn't mean being a Christian is like being a doormat. God is saying don't seek to do bodily harm or hurt people who have inflicted injury and got away. We shouldn't go looking for them in order to get revenge.

But whether they're arrested or not, we're tempted to think they won't get the punishment they deserve unless we take matters into our own hands. For example, if an intruder breaks into our house to steal in the middle of the night, that gives us the right to defend ourselves. If we grab a gun to deal with the intruder and they flee, that's fine. But if we chase after them and gun them down, we are no longer defending ourselves but seeking revenge. Look at it like this. If that same intruder has a gun, and I announce, "I have a weapon: I want you to leave," but the intruder starts shooting, if we then fire on the intruder to defend our family, that's not seeking revenge. We're protecting ourselves, our family and ensuring justice.

These are strange times we live in. We can easily speak up when others are doing us wrong. We don't just suffer silently and say, "God will get them." We're free to speak up. God wants people to turn from their wicked ways, repent and be saved. We have to witness to them. However, in regular conversations, if after talking with people who complicate things and try to make matters worse, we have to learn to separate ourselves. When we see others doing wrong to those who can't speak up for themselves, we should speak up. If we can reasonably reconcile with people, then we pray for them and keep life moving. If we can't reconcile with them, we pray and keep life moving. Notice: this time, we've removed *them* from the equation. The Bible says, "Can two walk together, unless they are agreed?" (Amos 3:3).

We have to learn the art of respectfully disagreeing to keep the main thing, the main thing. Otherwise, some will prey on you rather than pray with you for reconciliation. Then they'll yell, "You're supposed to be a Christian!" We become a doormat if we tolerate their wrongdoing and bad attitudes and don't speak up. We don't have to use profanity and cuss people out. We can agree to disagree peacefully. If at all possible, we can defend ourselves and not harm others. "If you let people treat you like a doormat, you'll be quite forgotten in the end" (Proverbs 29:21).

Daily Note Acumen—DNA Questions

Have you ever had a disagreement with someone and didn't speak up for yourself? If so, what was your reason for not speaking up? Do you feel like a doormat? Do you frequently let people walk all over you? Have you ever had to go back and communicate with someone you were in disagreement with? How did you handle it? Was the relationship mended or further broken? Examine whether there is something that you could have done differently. If there is, go back for some open dialogue with the people involved. Find out if things can be mended. You just may be the glue.

Have you ever had to defend yourself physically? If so, was there bodily harm or violence involved? What was the outcome for the party that was wrong, whether it was you or them? If it was you, have you confessed and repented? If it was them, did the situation allow you to forgive and move on? If you haven't forgiven them, do you plan on it?

If not, pray and consult with God to see what your next steps should be. Seek counseling if necessary and if the issue is affecting your mental health.

49.
FROM YOUR
MOUTH TO GOD'S
HEART

Now we know that God does not hear sinners; but if anyone is a worshiper of God and does His will, He hears him.

John 9:31

We don't have to walk our life's journey alone. We are given an opportunity to walk with Jesus. At some point, everyone has likely had somebody tell them about Jesus—whether they wanted to hear about Him or not. Some repeat His name in their everyday conversations as if it has no meaning. Some cry out to Him every day as if their life has no meaning. Then there are some who worship Him, sing praise unto His holy name and acknowledge Him in all of their ways.

It's hard to talk to someone we don't know. We don't normally walk right up and talk to strangers. Well, at least some of us don't. I, on the other hand, can't seem to help myself. I try the spirit by the Spirit to see what kind of conversation I should have with a stranger, always keeping in mind that I need to be about my Father's business. If I don't stop and say something when I felt I could have but was in a hurry, I normally feel bad later and ask God to forgive me. I don't want to take for granted that everyone has a personal relationship with God.

On more than one occasion, God has made me aware that He's listening. Not like He has a listening device planted on me, more like He has a direct, divine connection in me through His Holy Spirit. It's fascinating to me that when I talk to God, so many times He's responded back. I often wonder, "Who else has this type of relationship with God?" I pray that all Christians do. But if for some reason there are some who don't, I pray that they will go deeper and learn to hear from God.

A relationship with God is available on a daily basis. If you desire to worship Him and do His Will when you talk to Him, He hears you. Not only does He hear you, but He will answer. Many wonder why they don't hear from God. The Bible states, "God does not hear sinners; but if anyone is a worshiper of God and does His will, He hears him." That doesn't mean God is not listening, He's just not at the beck and call of sinners. God desires for those who worship Him to do it in spirit and truth. When we become true worshippers, we can talk to God and reach His heart.

The story of Hezekiah is a profound Bible story which illustrates the idea of something going from our mouth to God's heart. When Hezekiah became sick and near-death, Isaiah the prophet delivered a message to Hezekiah from God: "Set your house in order, for you shall die and not live" (2 Kings 20:1). Hezekiah turned his face to the wall, prayed to God and asked God to remember how he had walked before God in truth and with a loyal heart. He wept bitterly like a baby to God and said that he had done what was good in God's sight. Before Isaiah could get too far from Hezekiah, God had him turn around and go back and tell Hezekiah, "I have heard your prayer, I have seen your tears; surely I will add to your days fifteen years." God healed Hezekiah and delivered him from his enemies. Hezekiah had been sick, but he recovered.

I fast forward to COVID-19 and think about how many have died of it. There were many who didn't die of it as well. It was astonishing to watch the numbers rise and wonder if any deaths could have been prevented. I believe the fear of the unknown paralyzed a lot of people's mindset. Although, I also wonder do people know the power God has given us to be healed and how He designed the body with all its functions. As true worshippers seeking to do God's will, when we are sick, it's appropriate to cry out to God and ask for healing. I can testify of that because I had COVID-19 and I cried out to God and He healed me. If it's not your time to die, expect to be healed. Regardless, know that to be absent from the body is to be present with the Lord. That's more healing than we can ask for. However, there's something about being a true worshipper and having a personal relationship with God that whatever you speak from your mouth, it reaches God's heart.

Daily Note Acumen—DNA Questions

Have you ever cried out to God and He heard you and answered? If so, build a faith file to refer to for times when you'll need to have faith in other areas. If not, have you thought about building a relationship with God? Do you know the difference between being a sinner and a worshiper of God? Here's my definition: A sinner is a person running toward sin; a worshiper of God is a person running away from sin toward God. The difference doesn't make a worshiper of God perfect but spiritually mature. If you haven't become spiritually mature, ask God to intervene. Pray the prayer of confession and believe in Romans 10:8–13.

50.
LOOK NEGATIVITY
IN THE FACE AND
REJECT IT

Reject a divisive man after the first and second admonition.

Titus 3:10

Here's the harsh reality that we face when it comes to negativity: it normally comes from somebody in our inner circle, our immediate culture or from this world we live in. We're surrounded by negativity every day, from what we face on the job to the grocery store parking lot. We know that we really don't want to deal with it at all, but how do we when it comes from those we love or are closest to us? We normally cope with negativity from our loved ones by praying for them and being totally honest with them.

I've always found it funny that there is a popular new slang word or phrase in the African American community every year. It doesn't matter if you live in the suburbs or in an urban area. No matter where you travel, you'll hear it in these different communities because the new word becomes a fad. I personally don't take to many of them anymore, especially this one: "That's Everything." No. God is Everything. There is one in the African American community that we probably will never get rid of: *Hater*. It's used to describe a person who talks and behaves negatively when they hear or see other people's success, goals they've achieved, where they live or what they drive.

It's easier to look negativity in the face and reject it when it comes from those who we personally know or are of African American descent. Whether joking or serious, when most African Americans have to deal with negativity from someone, they will look the person right in the face and call them a hater. It becomes harder to reject negativity with those we don't have a personal relationship with or when we seek to avoid negative or corrupt communication. Most of us have hopes and dreams. At some point, we've probably shared our hopes and dreams with others only to be faced with their negativity. We may have shared with others, and they've offered no encouragement and could only tell us why our dream will not come to pass.

Those of us who have shared the gospel with others have experienced those who don't have enough faith to believe God can make a difference in their life. Negativity goes so deep in this world, and we know we can't banish it all. There will be negative things that keep occurring until Jesus returns, but we must keep the faith! When God wakes us up each day, most of us have a choice about how we will spend our day and plan our lives. We can pray for God's direction, mercy and help. Some of us have made the determination that we will allow Jesus to live through us. We've made the commitment and have the dedication to believe God's Word and actively practice it in our life. Our thoughts are on what will please God and how we can live a better life through Jesus Christ.

No matter what we have to go through or what we see going wrong in this world, we're determined to **look negativity in the face and reject it.** Not everyone will allow themselves the autonomy to confront negativity. It can be frightening to tell someone directly that they always seem negative. We run the risk of losing family and friends when we're honest with them about their negativity. Nevertheless, we should remind them that God's Word admonishes us to fill our minds with positivity and to meditate on true, noble, reputable, authentic and gracious things. We need to think about the best and not the worst. We can spend our time encouraging others to be the best they can be by seeing the beauty in everything and not the negativity.

Daily Note Acumen—DNA

Have you ever had to face negativity? Did it come from someone close to you or a stranger? Be totally honest with yourself: would most classify you as positive or negative? If negative, explore habits that cause you to be negative. Try thinking about what you'll say before you say it.

Do you have hopes and dreams that you share with others? Do they offer you encouragement or respond with negativity? Make a habit of only sharing your dreams and vision with those who are positive and reinforce positivity in you. Examine your inner circle and see if there are negative people in it. If there are, think about how to effectively communicate to them about their negativity. Do it in a way that will hopefully make the relationship better. If the negativity continues after one or two warnings, look it in the face and reject it.

CONCLUSION

It matters how you maneuver through life and whether you use the sword gifted to you by Jesus dying on the cross for your sins and the sins of the world. To cut through the intense layers of life that can distort your thinking or keep you from a successful journey to heaven, you will need to keep your sword sharp. It doesn't matter if you end up with cuts, scars and bruises, just as long as you make it. Don't leave God out of your decision-making process. Put on the whole armor of God and keep your sword on you at all times. God has instructed us to hide it in our hearts so that we don't sin against Him. Imagine that—it's a dagger to the heart that keeps one alive.

I pray that this book blesses you on your journey. I admonish you to get to know God. He's so AMAZING! Talk every area of your life over with Him, then trust that He has your best interests at heart. I'm just one example of God's transforming power. He took control of my life when I gave it to Him. I have no regrets, as it served the very purpose that it was destined to serve—for me to be able to teach and preach the Kingdom of God as a servant well-equipped to carry His Word and not back down when the enemy lodges attacks. I was under attack but not under siege. The enemy thought he had me captured, but through God, I escaped.

We have to continue the fight, but the battle belongs to God. He will equip you for the journey if you give your life to Him and keep your hands in His hands. You can be a light in this dark world, but not without your sword sharpened day by day. Don't look back, harbor no regrets! You will either break through or break down: it's your choice to make. You can make it if you can take it. When it's God's to call and ours to come, hopefully, I will see you at the mountain-top!

Grace and Peace,
Evangelist Shelly Lockett

Evangelist Shelly Lockett is available for in-person and virtual speaking events.

For more information, inspirational blog posts, and fun *Sharpen Your Sword* merchandise, please visit:

ShellyLockettMinistries.com

Connect with Evangelist Lockett on social media:

 kansas.phoenix

 @TheWordRules

 @LadyLockettKC

Made in the USA
Columbia, SC
28 April 2021